Henry L. Gilmour

Silver Trumpet

a collection of new and selected hymns - for use in public worship, revival services,

prayer and social meetings, and Sunday schools

Henry L. Gilmour

Silver Trumpet

a collection of new and selected hymns - for use in public worship, revival services, prayer and social meetings, and Sunday schools

ISBN/EAN: 9783337286255

Printed in Europe, USA, Canada, Australia, Japan

Cover: Foto ©Lupo / pixelio.de

More available books at **www.hansebooks.com**

THE

SILVER TRUMPET

A COLLECTION OF

NEW AND SELECTED HYMNS;

FOR USE IN

Public Worship, Revival Services, Prayer and Social Meetings, and Sunday Schools,

EDITED BY

Dr. H. L. GILMOUR and Capt. R. KELSO CARTER.

"And the Lord spake unto Moses, saying, Make thee two TRUMPETS of SILVER: that thou mayest use them for the calling of the assembly, and for the journeying of the camps. . . . to blow an alarm. . . . Also in the day of your gladness, and in your solemn days, and in the beginnings of your months, over your burnt-offerings, and over the sacrifices of your peace-offerings; that they may be to you for a memorial before your God."—Numbers i. 1-10.

Philadelphia: JOHN J. HOOD, 1018 Arch St.

Copyright, 1889, by John J. Hood.

Price, 35 cents per copy (postage prepaid); $3.60 per dozen (not prepaid).

INTRODUCTION.

IF Solomon could say in his day, "of making many books there is no end," what would he say if he could come back and stay with us *long enough* to look over the list of the publications of the present age?

That we are making many books is especially true in the department of christian song. But the Songsters of Zion are noted for their *bigness* of heart, and they are ever ready to welcome one more into the number that with melodious songs invite sinners to Jesus, and press believers to penetrate the Beulah land of religious experience.

Silver is a precious metal, and if it be pure, has melody in its ring. Silver is an old commodity, and the trumpet is an old instrument, and THE SILVER TRUMPET will not forget the old notes that cheered the hearts of pilgrims in days of yore. But the silver has gone through new processes of refinement, and the trumpet has had such additions and improvements as will enable THE SILVER TRUMPET of to-day to bring forth things that ARE NEW, as well as to perpetuate the best from the old treasuries of song.

About a year ago I wrote to Dr. Gilmour, earnestly requesting him to prepare a book of intensely spiritual songs, such as would give to the Christian world the benefit of his experience as a leader of singing at camp meetings, Sabbath-schools, and in revival services. I hail with special delight the appearance of THE SILVER TRUMPET, which so richly meets the great need that I had in mind when I wrote to him.

It was indeed a happy thought in the Doctor to make Rev. R. Kelso Carter an associate in this blessed service, and thus give us the benefit of his experience in the same line of christian work. On the baptism of the Holy Ghost THE SILVER TRUMPET gives no uncertain sound, and we doubt not but its echoes will be heard far on in the years to come. So may it be.

JOHN THOMPSON.

We would respectfully call attention to the classified arrangement of the hymns in THE SILVER TRUMPET, a departure which we believe will be hailed with approval by all who are interested in the direction and management of religious meetings. Pastors and evangelists will find this feature of the book of great practical value.

CHRISTIAN WORK,	Nos. 1 to 23.
THE HOLY SPIRIT,	Nos. 24 to 42.
CONSECRATION,	Nos. 43 to 62.
CHRISTIAN LIFE,	Nos. 63 to 155.
INVITATION,	Nos. 156 to 187.
FAMILIAR HYMNS,	Nos. 188 to 209.

By special arrangement we are able to include in this collection many of the best hymns of Jno. R. Sweney and Wm. J. Kirkpatrick, the well known and popular composers.

H. L. GILMOUR.
R. KELSO CARTER.

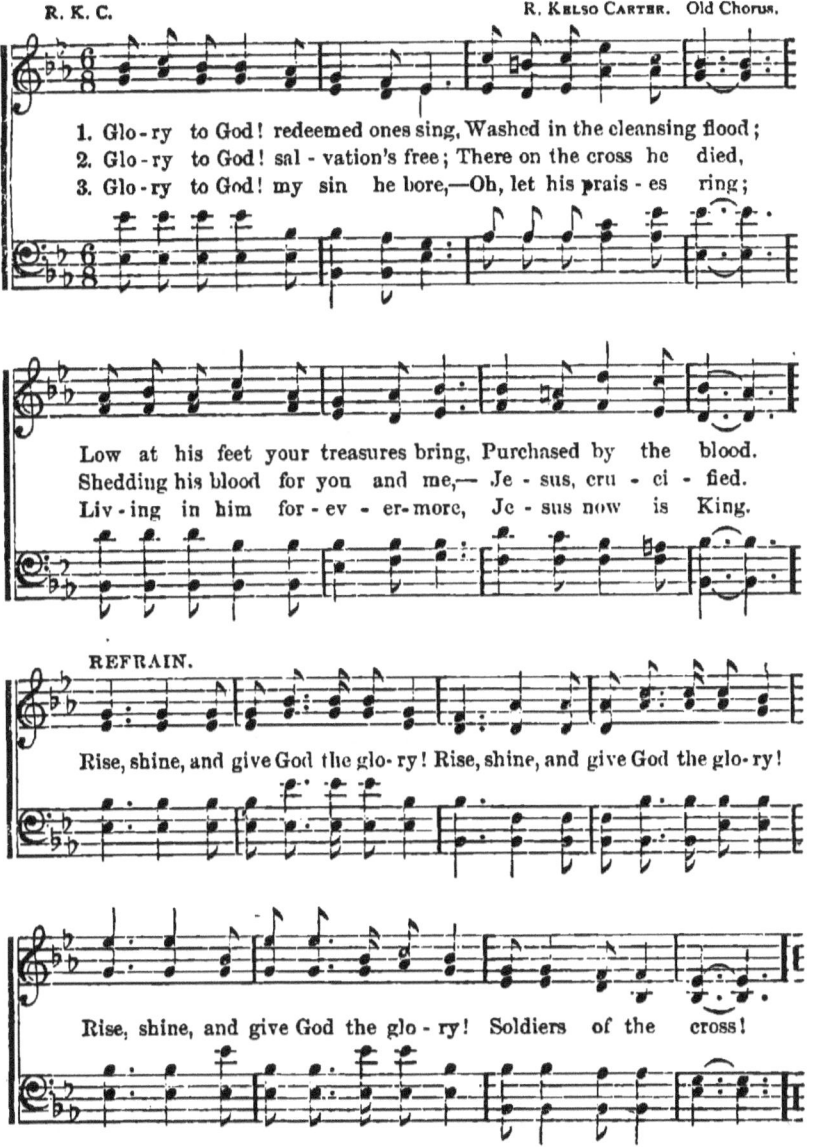

4 Glory to God! along the way
Freely the rivers flow;
Cleansing and keeping day by day
Whiter than the snow.

5 Glory to God the Father, and
Glory to God the Son!
Glory to God the Holy Ghost,
Mighty Three in One.

In His Name.

Lidie E. Hewitt.   Dedicated to "The King's Daughters."   Wm. J. Kirkpatrick.

1. Let us give the cup of wa-ter In His name; Help our Father's son or daughter In His name.
2. Let us pray for one an-oth-er In His name; Lift-ing up the fallen brother In His name.
3. With the love of Christ constraining, In His name, Work or bear without complaining, In His name.

REFRAIN.
In His name, oh, let the watch-word Blazoned on . . . our banners be; . . . Where the gleaming standard leads us, Let us fol-low loy-al-ly.

4 Let our lives flow out in blessing,
    In His name;
Bravely God's own truth confessing,
    In His name.

5 This will lighten every duty,
    In His name;
Fill our lives with heaven's beauty,
    In His name.

10. Onward, Christian Soldiers!

Sabine Baring-Gould. Tune, ONWARD. 6, 5.

1. Onward, Christian soldiers! Marching as to war, With the cross of Jesus Going on be-fore. Christ, the royal Mas-ter, Leads against the foe; Forward into bat-tle, See, his banners go!
2. At the sign of triumph Satan's host doth flee; On, then, Christian soldiers, On to vic-to-ry! Hell's foundations qiv-er At the shout of praise; Brothers, lift your voices, Loud your anthems raise.
3. Like a mighty army Moves the Church of God; Brothers, we are treading Where the saints have trod; We are not di-vid-ed, All one bo-dy we, One in hope and doctrine, One in chari-ty.

CHORUS.

Onward, Christian soldiers! Marching as to war, With the cross of Je-sus Going on be-fore.

4 Crowns and thrones may perish,
  Kingdoms rise and wane,
But the Church of Jesus
  Constant will remain;
Gates of hell can never
  'Gainst that Church prevail;
We have Christ's own promise,
  And that cannot fail.

5 Onward, then, ye people!
  Join our happy throng,
Blend with ours your voices
  In the triumph-song;
Glory, laud, and honor
  Unto Christ the King,
This through countless ages
  Men and angels sing.

12. Glorious Victory.

Fanny J. Crosby.   Wm. J. Kirkpatrick.

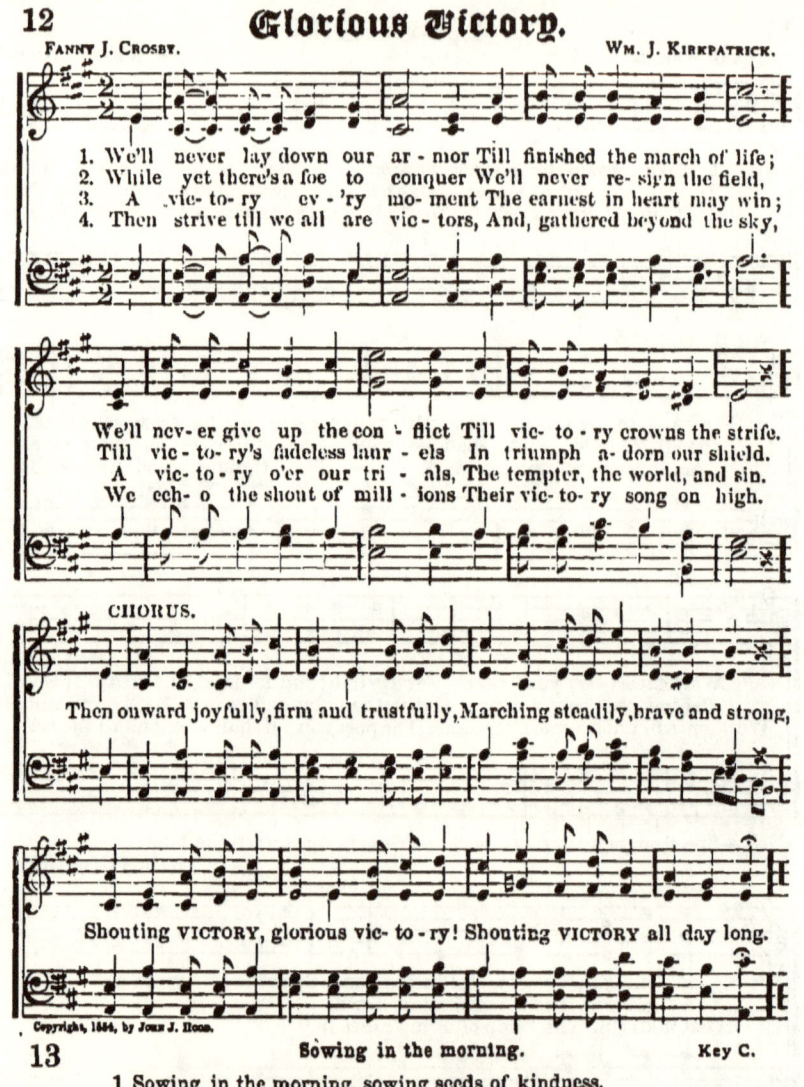

1. We'll never lay down our ar-mor Till finished the march of life;
2. While yet there's a foe to conquer We'll never re-sign the field,
3. A vic-to-ry ev-'ry mo-ment The earnest in heart may win;
4. Then strive till we all are vic-tors, And, gathered beyond the sky,

We'll nev-er give up the con-flict Till vic-to-ry crowns the strife.
Till vic-to-ry's fadeless laur-els In triumph a-dorn our shield.
A vic-to-ry o'er our tri-als, The tempter, the world, and sin.
We ech-o the shout of mill-ions Their vic-to-ry song on high.

CHORUS.

Then onward joyfully, firm and trustfully, Marching steadily, brave and strong,

Shouting VICTORY, glorious vic-to-ry! Shouting VICTORY all day long.

Copyright, 1884, by John J. Hood.

13. Sowing in the morning.   Key C.

1 Sowing in the morning, sowing seeds of kindness,
Sowing in the noon-tide, and the dewy eves;
Waiting for the harvest, and the time of reaping, We shall come, etc.

Cho.—Bringing in the sheaves, :|| We shall come rejoicing, bringing in the sheaves.

2 Sowing in the sunshine, sowing in the shadows,
Fearing neither clouds nor winter's chilling breeze;
By and by the harvest, and the labor ended, We shall come, etc.

3 Go, then, ever weeping, sowing for the Master,
Though the loss sustained our spirit often grieves,
When our weeping's over, he will bid us welcome, We shall come, etc.

14 The Morning Light.

Samuel F. Smith.   Tune, WEBB. 7, 6.

D.S. 1 The morning light is breaking;
 The darkness disappears;
 The sons of earth are waking
 To penitential tears;
 Each breeze that sweeps the ocean
 Brings tidings from afar,
 Of nations in commotion,
 Prepared for Zion's war.

2 See heathen nations bending
 Before the God we love,
 And thousand hearts ascending
 In gratitude above;
 While sinners, now confessing,
 The gospel call obey,
 And seek the Saviour's blessing,
 A nation in a day.

3 Blest river of salvation,
 Pursue thine onward way;
 Flow thou to every nation,
 Nor in thy richness stay:
 Stay not till all the lowly
 Triumphant reach their home:
 Stay not till all the holy
 Proclaim, "The Lord is come!"

15   Geo. Duffield, Jr.   Stand up, stand up for Jesus.   Tune above.

1 Stand up, stand up for Jesus,
 Ye soldiers of the cross;
 Lift high his royal banner,
 It must not suffer loss;
 From victory unto victory
 His army shall he lead
 Till every foe is vanquished
 And Christ is Lord indeed.

2 Stand up, stand up for Jesus,
 The trumpet call obey;
 Forth to the mighty conflict,
 In this his glorious day:
 "Ye that are men, now serve him,"
 Against unnumbered foes;
 Your courage rise with danger,
 And strength to strength oppose.

3 Stand up, stand up for Jesus,
 Stand in his strength alone;
 The arm of flesh will fail you;
 Ye dare not trust your own:
 Put on the gospel armor,
 Each piece put on with prayer;
 Where duty calls, or danger,
 Be never wanting there.

4 Stand up, stand up for Jesus,
 The strife will not be long;
 This day the noise of battle,
 The next the victor's song:
 To him that overcometh,
 A crown of life shall be;
 He with the King of glory
 Shall reign eternally.

16   Work, for the night is coming.   Key F.

1 Work, for the night is coming,
 Work through the morning hours;
 Work, while the dew is sparkling,
 Work 'mid springing flowers;
 Work, when the day grows brighter,
 Work in the glowing sun;
 Work, for the night is coming,
 When man's work is done.

2 Work, for the night is coming;
 Work through the sunny noon;
 Fill brightest hours with labor;
 Rest comes sure and soon.

Give every flying minute
 Something to keep in store;
 Work for the night is coming,
 When man works no more.

3 Work for the night is coming,
 Under the sunset skies;
 While their bright tints are glowing,
 Work, for daylight flies.
 Work till the last beam fadeth,
 Fadeth to shine no more;
 Work while the night is darkening,
 When man's work is o'er.

17. Soldiers of the Cross.

J. B WATERBURY.   Tune, CALEDONIA. 7, 7, 7, 6.

1. Soldiers of the cross, arise! Lo! your Leader from the skies
Waves before you glory's prize, The prize of victory.
Seize your armor, gird it on; Now the battle will be won;
See, the strife will soon be done; Then struggle manfully.

2. Now the fight of faith begin, Be no more the slaves of sin.
Strive the victor's palm to win, Trusting in the Lord:
Gird ye on the armor bright, Warriors of the King of Light,
Never yield, nor lose by flight Your divine reward.

3 Jesus conquered when he fell,
Met and vanquished earth and hell;
Now he leads you on to swell
  The triumphs of his cross.
Though all earth and hell appear,
Who will doubt, or who can fear?
God, our strength and shield, is near;
  We cannot lose our cause.

4 Onward, then, ye hosts of God!
Jesus points the victor's rod;
Follow where your Leader trod;
  You soon shall see his face.
Soon, your enemies all slain,
Crowns of glory you shall gain,
Soon you'll join that glorious train
  Who shout their Saviour's praise.

18. Fly to the Rescue.

ABBIE MILLS.   Acts xxvii. 43.   H. L. GILMOUR.

1. Fly to the res-cue! danger's nigh, Precious souls 'mid breakers die;
2. Fly to the res-cue! sin-ners sleep There up-on the treacherous deep;
3. Fly to the res-cue! tempest-tossed Those that priceless treasure cost,

Snatch them from the rag-ing foam; Je-sus wants them in his home.
Dash-ing now 'mid rocks and shoals; Fly to save these shipwrecked souls.
See the blood on Cal-vary flow And the wealth en-dangered know.

CHORUS.
Fly to the res-cue! lend a hand! To the res-cue, val-iant band!
Quick! man the life-boat, like sailors brave! Jesus bids; he waits to save!

4 Fly to the rescue! hear the moan
Where the Spirit's light hath shone
O'er the death that never dies
"Saviour help!" the lost one cries,

5 Fly to the rescue! Jesus hears;
On the waves he now appears;
Will you walk beside him there?
Learn how sweet is answered prayer?

6 Fly to the rescue! sin's forgiven;
Raise the sinking souls to heaven;
Hear them shout deliverence now,
While at Jesus' feet they bow.

7 Fly to the rescue! storms all o'er,
We shall stand on yonder shore
'Mid a countless, ransomed throng,
Singing there salvation's song.

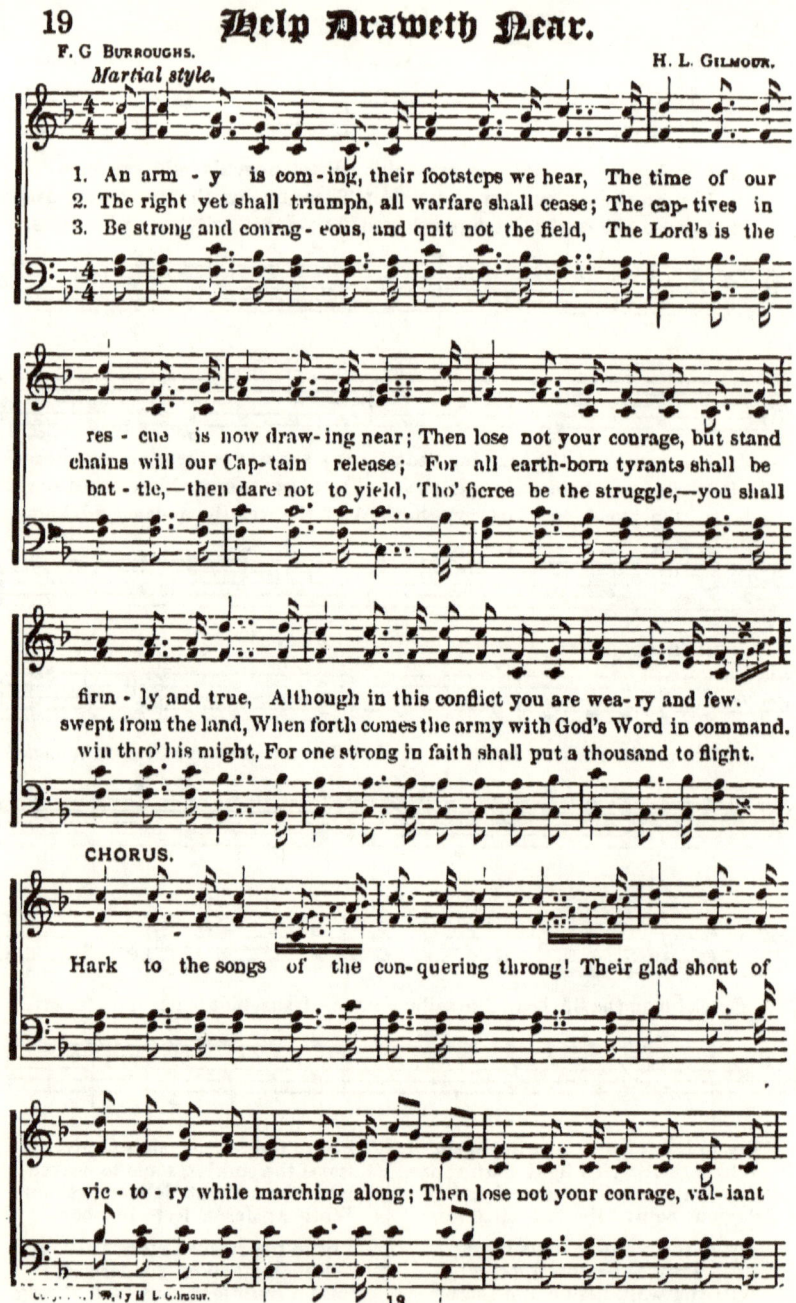

Help Draweth Near.—CONCLUDED.

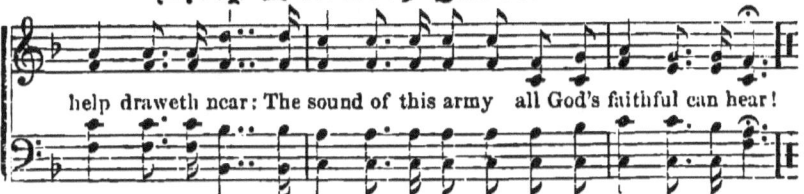

Laban. S. M.

20   A charge to keep I have.

1 A charge to keep I have,
  A God to glorify,
  A never-dying soul to save,
  And fit it for the sky.

2 To serve the present age,
  My calling to fulfill,—
  Oh, may it all my powers engage,
  To do my Master's will.

3 Arm me with jealous care,
  As in thy sight to live;
  And oh, thy servant, Lord, prepare,
  A strict account to give.

4 Help me to watch and pray,
  And on thyself rely,
  Assured, if I my trust betray
  I shall forever die. —C. Wesley.

21   My soul, be on thy guard.

1 My soul, be on thy guard;
  Ten thousand foes arise;
  The hosts of sin are pressing hard
  To draw thee from the skies.

2 Oh, watch, and fight, and pray;
  The battle ne'er give o'er;
  Renew it boldly every day,
  And help divine implore.

3 Ne'er think the victory won,
  Nor lay thine armor down:
  The work of faith will not be done
  Till thou obtain the crown.

4 Fight on, my soul, till death
  Shall bring thee to thy God;
  He'll take thee, at thy parting breath,
  To his divine abode. —G. Heath.

22   Equip me for the war.

1 Equip me for the war,
  And teach my hands to fight;
  My simple, upright heart prepare,
  And guide my words aright.

2 Control my every thought,
  My whole of sin remove;
  Let all my works in thee be wrought,
  Let all be wrought in love.

3 O arm me with the mind,
  Meek Lamb, that was in thee;
  And let my knowing zeal be joined
  With perfect charity.

4 With calm and tempered zeal
  Let me enforce thy call;
  And vindicate thy gracious will,
  Which offers life to all. —C. Wesley.

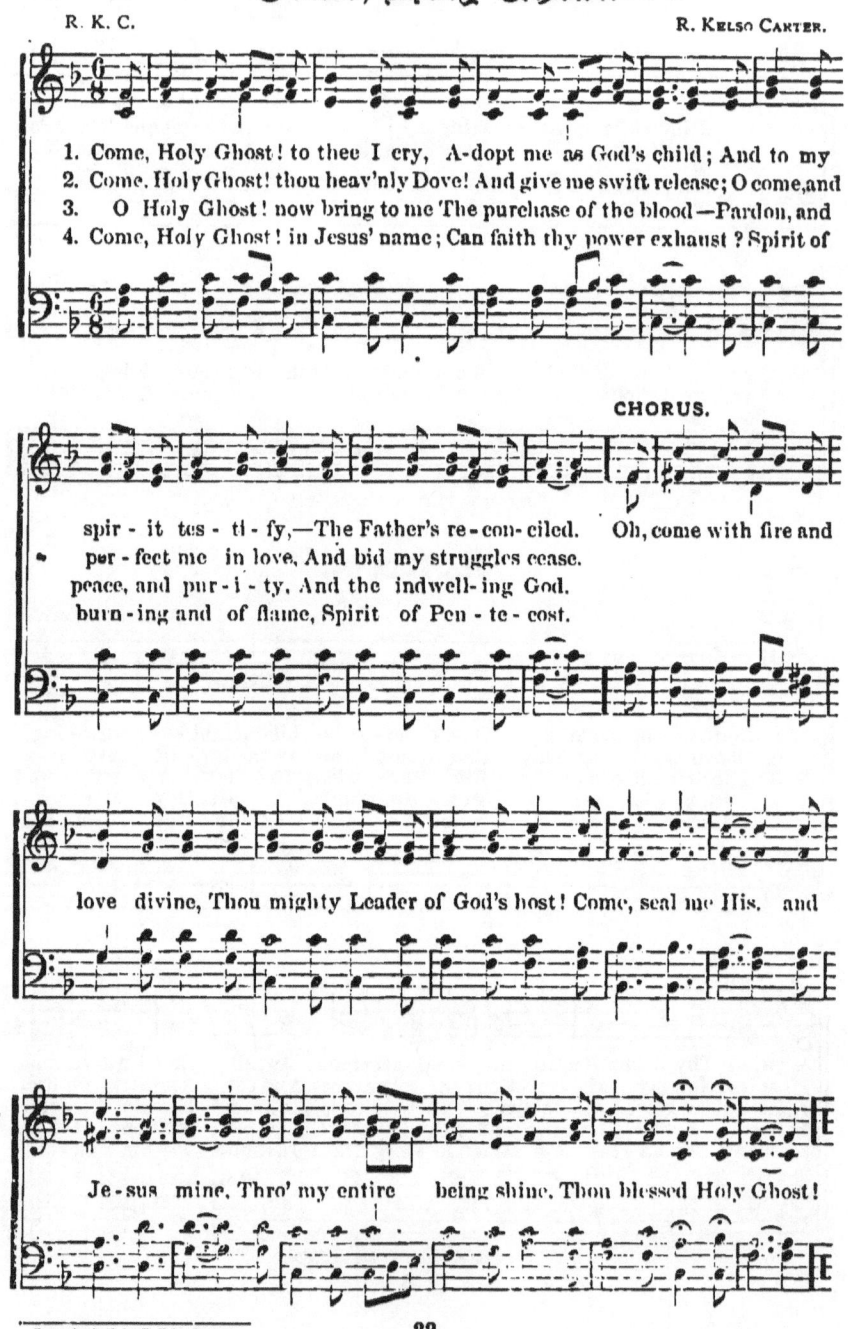

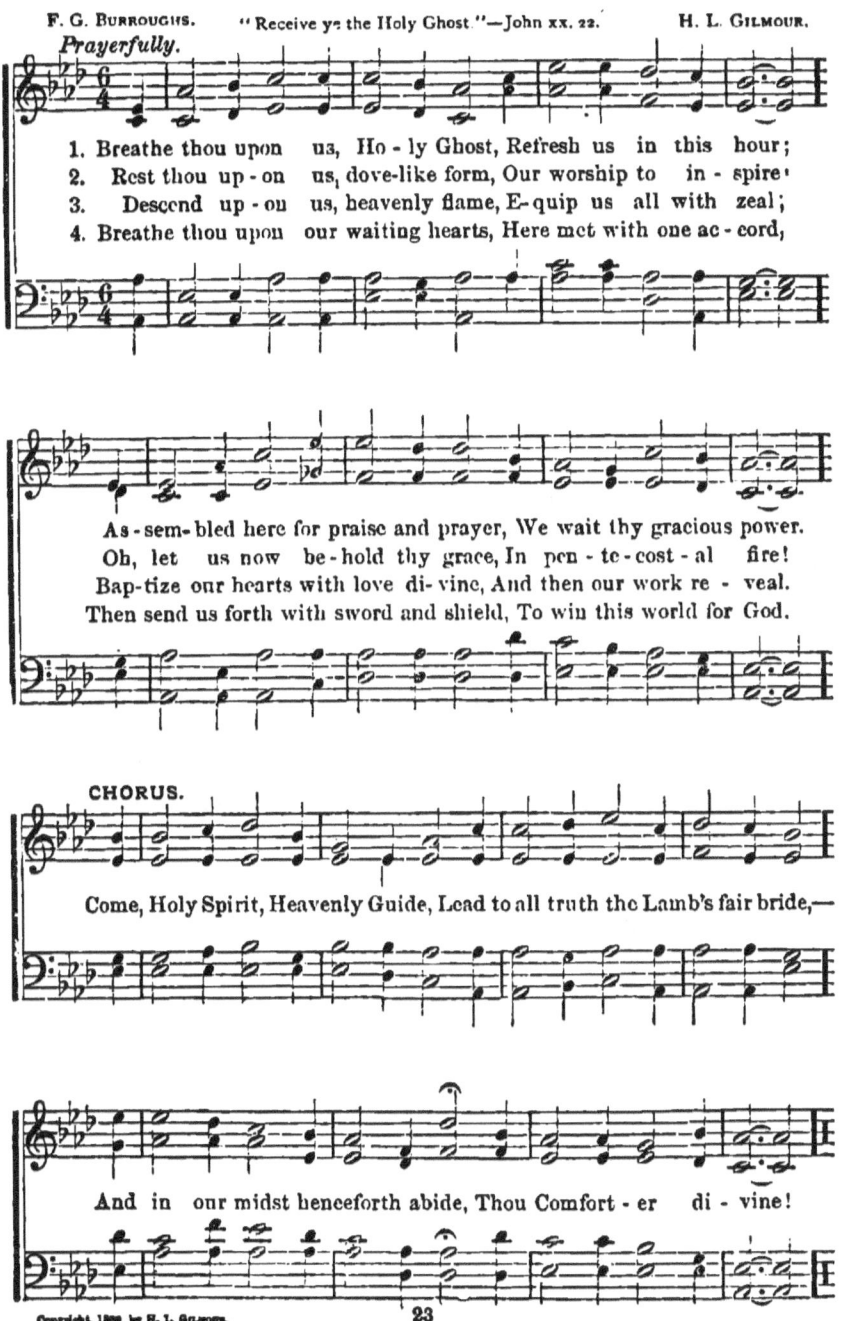

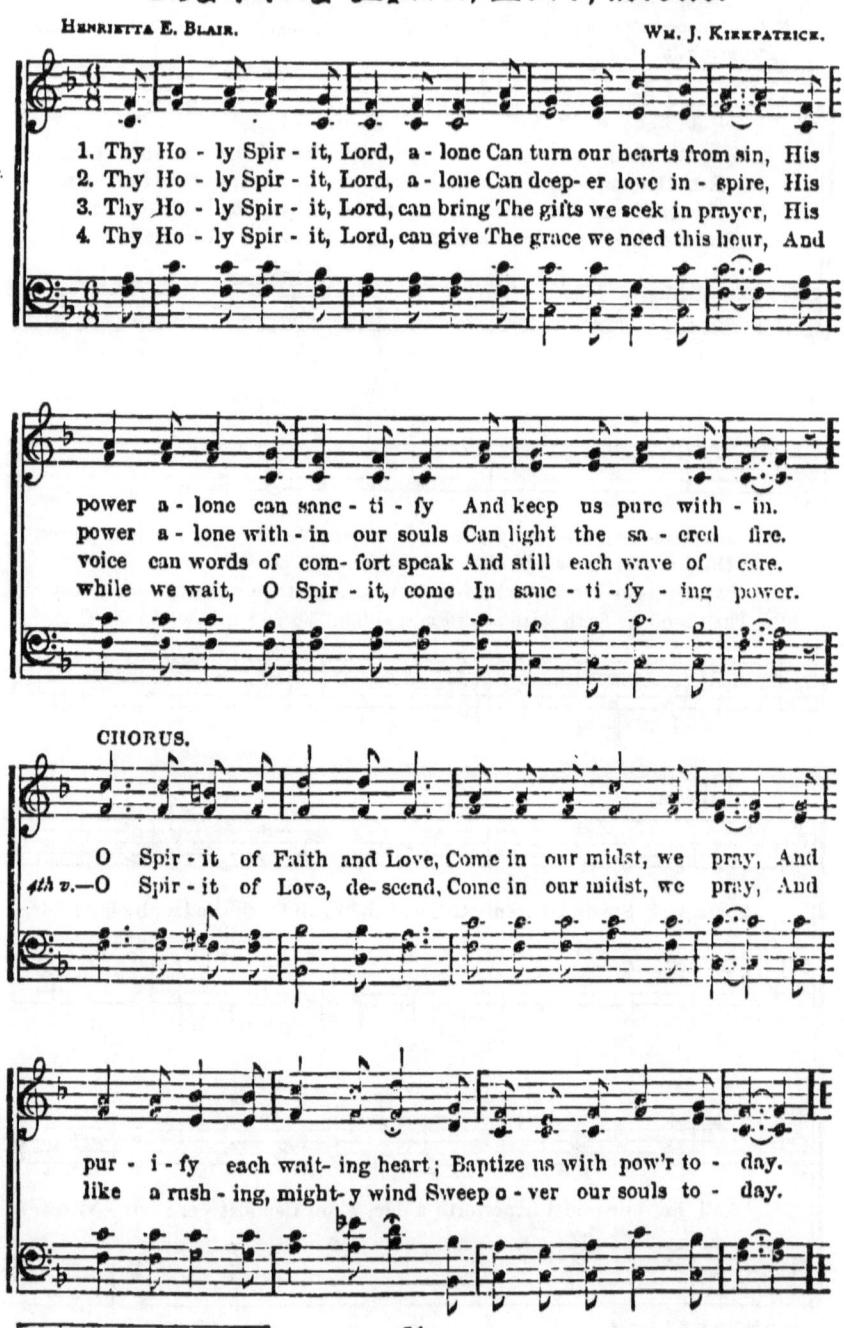

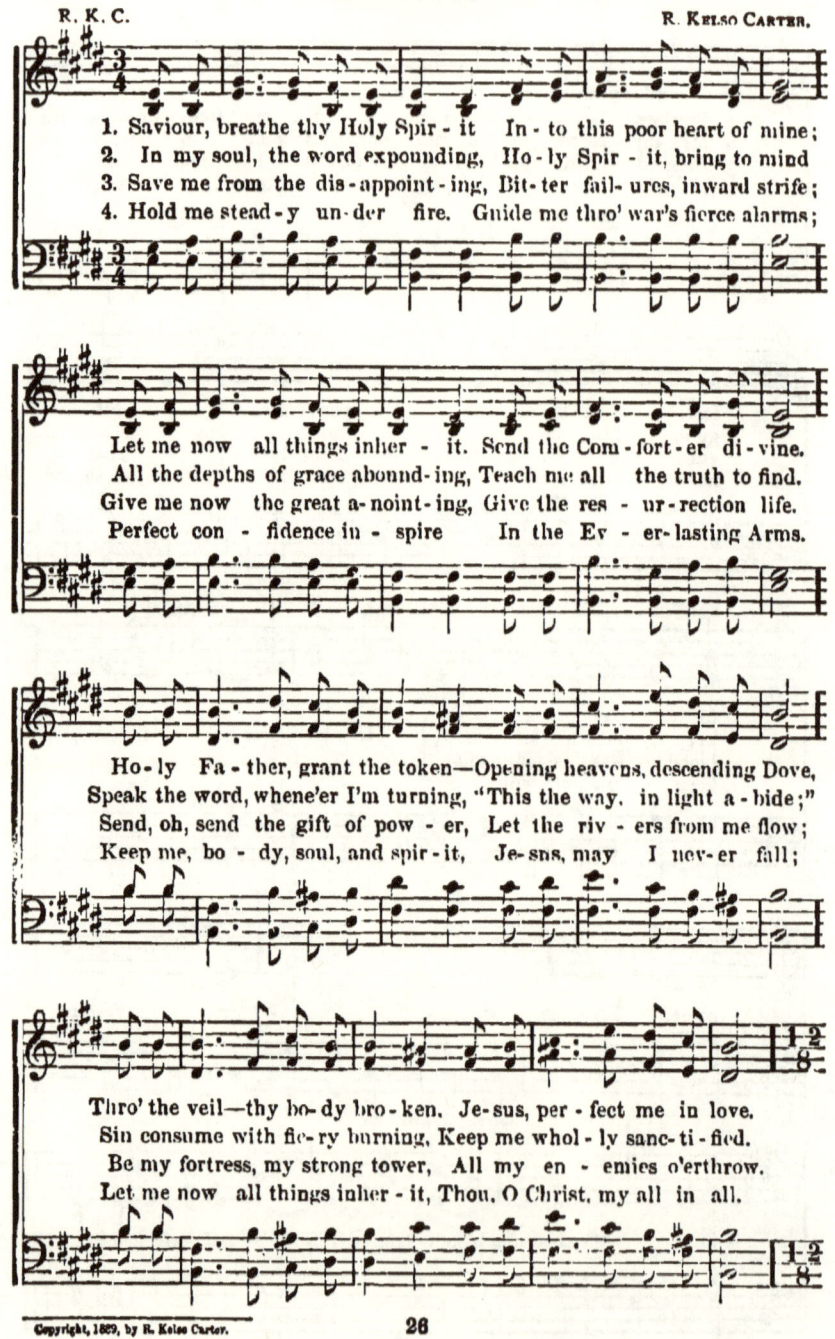

Comforter.—CONCLUDED.

30. Now I feel the Sacred Fire.

Arranged by R. Kelso Carter.

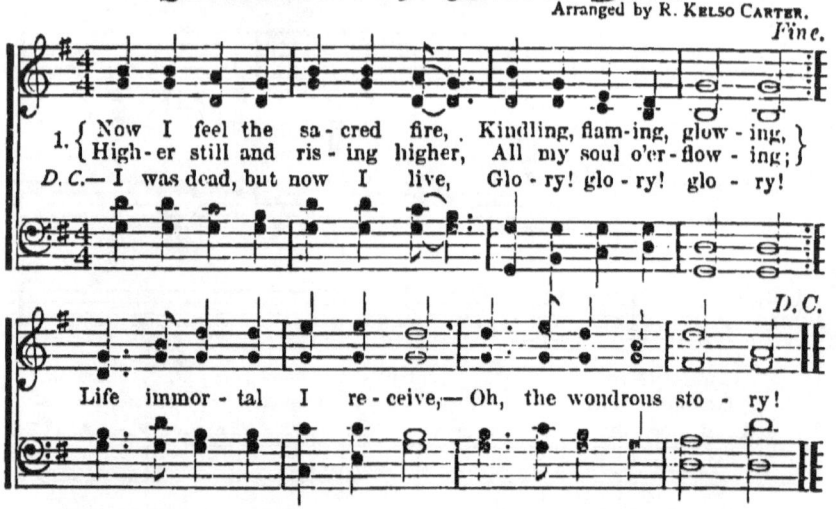

1. Now I feel the sa-cred fire, Kindling, flaming, glowing,
   Higher still and rising higher, All my soul o'er-flowing;
D.C.— I was dead, but now I live, Glory! glory! glory!
Life immortal I receive,— Oh, the wondrous story!

2 Now I am from bondage freed,
    Every bond is riven;
  Jesus makes me free indeed,
    Just as free as heaven:
  'Tis a glorious liberty—
    Oh, the wondrous story!
  I was bound, but now I'm free,
    Glory! glory! glory!

3 Let the testimony roll,
    Roll through every nation;
  Witnessing from soul to soul,
    This immense salvation,
  Now I know it's full and free;
    Oh, the wondrous story!
  For I feel it saving me,
    Glory! glory! glory!

4 Glory be to God on high,
    Glory be to Jesus!
  He hath brought salvation nigh,
    From all sin he frees us.
  Let the golden harps of God
    Ring the wondrous story;
  Let the pilgrim shout aloud,
    Glory! glory! glory!

5 Let the trump of jubilee,
    The glad tidings thunder;
  Jesus sets the captives free:
    Bursts their bonds asunder;
  Fetters break and dungeons fall,
    Oh, the wondrous story!
  This salvation's free to all,
    Glory! glory! glory!

Copyright, 1886, by John J. Hood.

31. Fill Me Now.

Rev. E. H. Stokes, D.D.   Jno. R. Sweney.

1. Hover o'er me, Holy Spirit; Bathe my trembling heart and brow;
2. Thou can'st fill me, gracious Spirit, Tho' I can-not tell thee how;
3. I am weakness, full of weakness; At thy sacred feet I bow.
4. Cleanse and comfort; bless and save me; Bathe, oh, bathe my heart and brow!

Fill Me Now.—CONCLUDED.

Fill me with thy hal-low'd presence, Come, oh, come and fill me now.
But I need thee, great-ly need thee, Come, oh, come and fill me now.
Blest, di-vine, e-ter-nal Spir-it, Fill with power, and fill me now.
Thou art comfort-ing and sav-ing, Thou art sweet-ly fill-ing now.

D.S. Fill me with thy hal-low'd presence,—Come, oh, come and fill me now.

CHORUS.

Fill me now, fill me now, Ho-ly Spir-it, and fill me now;

COPYRIGHT, 1879, by JOHN J. HOOD.

32 O for that Flame.

BATHURST. Tune, SESSIONS.

1. O for that flame of living fire, Which shone so bright in saints of old;

Which bade their souls to heaven aspire,—Calm in distress, in danger bold.

2 Where is that Spirit, Lord, which dwelt
  In Abrah'm's breast, and sealed him
    thine?   [melt.
Which made Paul's heart with sorrow
And glow with energy divine?—

3 That Spirit, which from age to age
  Proclaimed thy love, and taught thy
Brightened Isaiah's vivid page, [ways?
And breathed in David's hallowed lays?

4 Is not thy grace as mighty now
  As when Elijah felt its power;
When glory beamed from Moses' brow,
Or Job endured the trying hour?

5 Remember, Lord, the ancient days;
  Renew thy work; thy grace restore;
And while to thee our hearts we raise,
On us thy Holy Spirit pour.

Pleyel's Hymn. 7s. — IGNACE PLEYEL.

33 Gracious Spirit, love divine.

1 GRACIOUS Spirit, love divine,
Let thy light within me shine!
All my guilty fears remove;
Fill me with thy heavenly love.

2 Speak thy pardoning grace to me;
Set the burdened sinner free;
Lead me to the Lamb of God;
Wash me in his precious blood.

3 Life and peace to me impart;
Seal salvation on my heart;
Breathe thyself into my breast,
Earnest of immortal rest.

4 Let me never from thee stray;
Keep me in the narrow way;
Fill my soul with joy divine;
Keep me, Lord, forever thine.

34 Holy Ghost, with light divine.

1 HOLY GHOST, with light divine,
Shine upon this heart of mine;
Chase the shades of night away,
Turn my darkness into day.

2 Holy Ghost, with power divine,
Cleanse this guilty heart of mine;
Long hath sin, without control,
Held dominion o'er my soul.

3 Holy Ghost, with joy divine,
Cheer this saddened heart of mine;
Bid my many woes depart,
Heal my wounded, bleeding heart.

4 Holy Spirit, all divine,
Dwell within this heart of mine;
Cast down every idol-throne,
Reign supreme—and reign alone.

Rockingham. L. M. — LOWELL MASON.

35   Lord, God, the Holy Ghost.

1 LORD, God, the Holy Ghost!
 In this accepted hour,
 As on the day of Pentecost,
 Descend in all thy power.

2 We meet with one accord
 In our appointed place,
 And wait the promise of our Lord,—
 The Spirit of all grace.

3 Like mighty, rushing wind
 Upon the waves beneath,
 Move with one impulse every mind;
 One soul, one feeling breathe.

4 The young, the old, inspire
 With wisdom from above; [fire,
 And give us hearts and tongues of
 To pray, and praise, and love.

5 Spirit of light! explore,
 And chase our gloom away,
 With luster shining more and more,
 Unto the perfect day.

36   Come, Holy Spirit, come.

1 COME, Holy Spirit, come,
 With energy divine,
 And on this poor, benighted soul
 With beams of mercy shine.

2 From the celestial hills
 Light, life, and joy dispense;
 And may I daily, hourly, feel
 Thy quickening influence.

3 O melt this frozen heart,
 This stubborn will subdue;
 Each evil passion overcome,
 And form me all anew.

4 The profit will be mine,
 But thine shall be the praise;
 Cheerful to thee will I devote
 The remnant of my days.

37   Come, Holy Spirit.
Tune, Rockingham, opposite page.

1 COME, Holy Spirit, raise our songs
 To reach the wonders of that day,
 When, with thy fiery, cloven tongues
 Thou didst such glorious scenes display.

2 Lord, we believe to us and ours,
 The apostolic promise given;
 We wait the pentecostal powers,
 The Holy Ghost sent down from heaven.

3 Assembled here with one accord,
 Calmly we wait the promised grace,
 The purchase of our dying Lord;
 Come, Holy Ghost, and fill the place.

4 If every one that asks, may find,
 If still thou dost on sinners fall,
 Come as a mighty, rushing wind;
 Great grace be now upon us all.

5 O leave us not to mourn below,
 Or long for thy return to pine;
 Now, Lord, the Comforter bestow,
 And fix in us the Guest divine.

38   O Spirit of the Living God.
Tune, Rockingham, opposite page.

1 O SPIRIT of the living God,
 In all thy plenitude of grace,
 Where'er the foot of man hath trod,
 Descend on our apostate race.

2 Give tongues of fire and hearts of love,
 To preach the reconciling word;
 Give power and unction from above,
 Where'er the joyful sound is heard.

3 Be darkness, at thy coming, light;
 Confusion—order, in thy path; [might;
 Souls without strength, inspire with
 Bid mercy triumph over wrath.

4 Baptize the nations; far and nigh
 The triumphs of the cross record;
 The name of Jesus glorify,
 Till every kindred call him Lord.

Azmon. C. M.

Carl Gotthelf Gläser.

39 Enthroned On High.

1 ENTHRONED on high, almighty Lord,
  The Holy Ghost send down;
  Fulfill in us thy faithful word,
  And all thy mercies crown.

2 Though on our heads no tongues of fire
  Their wondrous powers impart,
  Grant, Saviour, what we more desire,—
  Thy Spirit in our heart.

3 Spirit of life, and light, and love,
  Thy heavenly influence give;
  Quicken our souls, our guilt remove,
  That we in Christ may live.

4 To our benighted minds reveal
  The glories of his grace,
  And bring us where no clouds conceal
  The brightness of his face.

5 His love within us shed abroad,
  Life's ever-springing well;
  Till God in us, and we in God,
  In love eternal dwell.
  —THOMAS HAWEIS.

40 Jesus, thine all-victorious.

1 JESUS, thine all-victorious love
  Shed in my heart abroad:
  Then shall my feet no longer rove,
  Rooted and fixed in God.

2 O that in me the sacred fire
  Might now begin to glow,
  Burn up the dross of base desire
  And make the mountains flow!

3 O that it now from heaven might fall,
  And all my sins consume!
  Come, Holy Ghost, for thee I call;
  Spirit of burning, come!

4 Refining fire, go through my heart;
  Illuminate my soul;
  Scatter thy life through every part,
  And sanctify the whole.

5 My steadfast soul, from falling free,
  Shall then no longer move,
  While Christ is all the world to me,
  And all my heart is love.
  —CHAS. WESLEY.

41 Jesus, My Life.

1 JESUS, my life, thyself apply,
  Thy Holy Spirit breathe:
  My vile affections crucify;
  Conform me to thy death.

2 Conqueror of hell and earth, and sin,
  Still with the rebel strive:
  Enter my soul, and work within,
  And kill, and make alive.

3 More of thy life, and more I have,
  As the old Adam dies;
  Bury me, Saviour, in thy grave,
  That I with thee may rise.

4 Reign in me, Lord; thy foes control,
  Who would not own thy sway;
  Diffuse thine image through my soul;
  Shine to thy perfect day.

5 Scatter the last remains of sin,
  And seal me thine abode;
  O make me glorious all within,
  A temple built by God!
  —CHAS. WESLEY.

42 I Worship Thee.

1 I WORSHIP thee, O Holy Ghost,
  I love to worship thee;
  My risen Lord for aye were lost
  But for thy company.

2 I worship thee, O Holy Ghost,
  I love to worship thee; [know'st
  I grieved thee long, alas! thou
  It grieves me bitterly,

3 I worship thee, O Holy Ghost,
  I love to worship thee;
  Thy patient love, at what a cost
  At last it conqured me!

4 I worship thee, O Holy Ghost,
  I love to worship thee;
  With thee each day is Pentecost,
  Each night Nativity,
  —W. F. WARREN.

43. Take My Life, and Let It Be.

Frances Ridley Havergal.
Cho. by R. K. C.

Old English, arranged.
Cho. by R. Kelso Carter.

1. Take my life, and let it be Con-secrat-ed, Lord, to thee;
2. Take my feet, and let them be Swift and beau-ti-ful for thee;
3. Take my lips, and let them be Filled with messag-es for thee;
4. Take my moments and my days, Let them flow in end-less praise;

Take my hands, and let them move At the im-pulse of thy love.
Take my voice, and let me sing Al-ways, on-ly, for my King.
Take my sil-ver and my gold,— Not a mite would I with-hold.
Take my in-tel-lect, and use Ev'-ry power as thou shalt choose.

CHORUS.

Take my spir-it, bo-dy, soul, Touch me, Lord, and make me whole;

Here am I, henceforth to be Con-se-crat-ed, Lord, to thee!

5 Take my will, and make it thine;
It shall be no longer mine;
Take my heart,—it is thine own,—
It shall be thy royal throne.

6 Take my love,—my Lord, I pour
At thy feet its treasure-store!
Take myself, and I will be
Ever, only, all for thee!

The Silver Trumpet-C

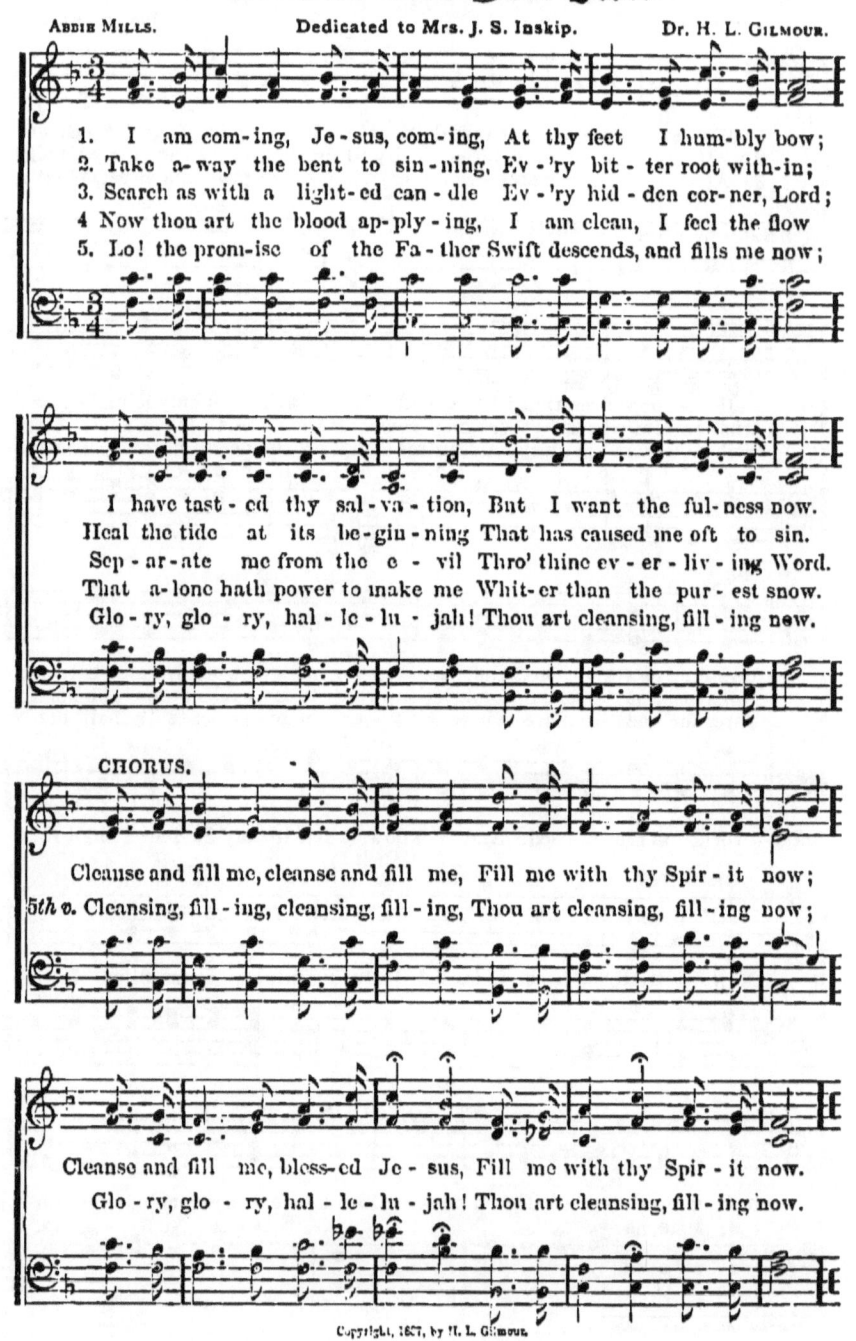

52. Victory.

Words arr. by H. L. G.
Dr. H. L. Gilmour.

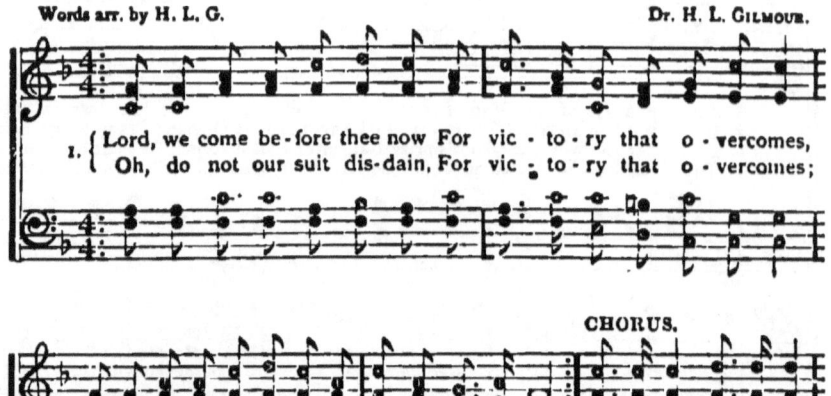

1. Lord, we come before thee now For victory that overcomes,
Oh, do not our suit disdain, For victory that overcomes;
At thy feet we humbly bow For vict'ry thro' the Lamb;
Shall we seek thee, Lord, in vain For vict'ry thro' the Lamb?

CHORUS.

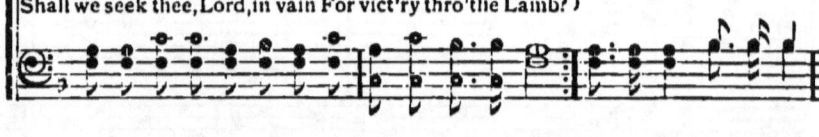

Victo-ry, vic-to-ry,

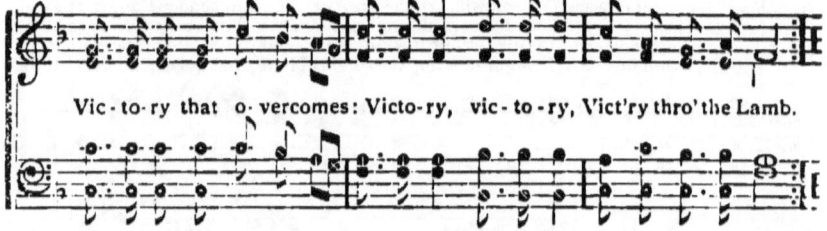

Vic-to-ry that o-vercomes: Victo-ry, vic-to-ry, Vict'ry thro' the Lamb.

2 Lord, on thee our souls depend
For victory that overcomes,
In compassion now descend,—
Give vict'ry thro' the Lamb;
Fill our hearts with thy rich grace,
And victory that overcomes,
Tune our lips to sing thy praise
For vict'ry thro' the Lamb.

3 Send some message from thy word,
And victory that overcomes,
That may joy and peace afford,
And vict'ry thro' the Lamb;
Let thy spirit now impart
A victory that overcomes,
Full salvation to each heart,
And vict'ry thro' the Lamb.

4 Comfort those who weep and mourn
For victory that overcomes,
Let the time of joy return,
And vict'ry thro' the Lamb;
Those that are cast down lift up
With victory that overcomes,
Make them strong in faith and hope,
And vict'ry thro' the Lamb.

5 Grant that all may seek and find
A victory that overcomes
Thee, a gracious God and kind,
And vict'ry thro' the Lamb;
Heal the sick, the captive free,
With victory that overcomes,
Let us all rejoice in thee
For vict'ry thro' the Lamb.

Copyright, 1853, by John J. Hood.

53. At the Cross.

R. Kelso Carter. From "Songs of Perfect Love," by per.

1. O Jesus, Lord, thy dying love Hath pierced my contrite heart;
2. Amid the night of sin and death Thy light hath filled my soul;
3. I kiss thy feet, I clasp thy hand, I touch thy bleeding side;
4. My Lord, my light, my strength, my all, I count my gain but loss.

Cho.—At the cross, at the cross, where I first saw the light,
And the burden of my heart rolled away,

Now take my life, and let me prove How dear to me thou art.
To me thy loving voice now saith, Thy faith hath made thee whole.
Oh, let me here forever stand, Where thou wast crucified.
Forever let thy love enthrall, And keep me at the cross.

It was there by faith I received my sight, And now I am happy night and day!

54. Vain, Delusive World.

C. Wesley. Tune, PENITENCE.

1. Vain, delusive world, adieu, With all of creature good! Only Jesus I pursue,
D.S.—Only Jesus will I know,

Fine.

Who bought me with his blood: All thy pleasures I forego;
And Jesus crucified. I trample on thy wealth and pride;

D.S.

2 Other knowledge I disdain;
'Tis all but vanity:
Christ, the Lamb of God, was slain,
He tasted death for me.
Me to save from endless woe
The sin-atoning Victim died:
Only Jesus will I know,
And Jesus crucified.

3 Here will I set up my rest;
My fluctuating heart
From the haven of his breast
Shall never more depart:
Whither should a sinner go?
His wounds for me stand open wide;
Only Jesus will I know,
And Jesus crucified.

4 Him to know is life and peace,
And pleasure without end;
This is all my happiness,
On Jesus to depend;
Daily in his grace to grow,
And ever in his faith abide;
Only Jesus will I know,
And Jesus crucified.

2 O that I could all invite,
This saving truth to prove;
Show the length, the breadth, the
And depth of Jesus' love! [height,
Fain I would to sinners show
The blood by faith alone applied;
Only Jesus will I know,
And Jesus crucified.

Forest. L. M.

55   O that my load of sin were gone.   L.M.

1 O that my load of sin were gone!,
O that I could at last submit
At Jesus' feet to lay it down—
To lay my soul at Jesus' feet!

2 Rest for my soul I long to find:
Saviour of all, if mine thou art,
Give me thy meek and lowly mind,
And stamp thine image on my heart.

3 Break off the yoke of inbred sin,
And fully set my spirit free;
I cannot rest till pure within,
Till I am wholly lost in thee.

4 Fain would I learn of thee, my God,
Thy light and easy burden prove,
The cross all stained with hallowed blood,
The labor of thy dying love.

5 I would, but thou must give the power;
My heart from every sin release;
Bring near, bring near the joyful hour,
And fill me with thy perfect peace.
—CHAS. WESLEY.

56   Lord, I am Thine.   L.M.

1 Lord, I am thine, entirely thine,
Purchased and saved by blood divine;
With full consent thine would I be,
And own thy sovereign right in me.

2 Thine would I live, thine would I die;
Be thine through all eternity;
The vow is past, beyond repeal,
And now I set the solemn seal.

3 Here, at that cross where flows the blood
That bought my guilty soul for God,
Thee, my new Master now I call,
And consecrate to thee my all.

4 Do thou assist a feeble worm
The great engagement to perform;
Thy grace can full assistance lend,
And on that grace I dare depend.
—SAMUEL DAVIES.

57   I thirst, Thou wounded Lamb of God.   L.M.

1 I thirst, thou wounded Lamb of God,
To wash me in thy cleansing blood;
To dwell within thy wounds; then pain
Is sweet, and life or death is gain.

2 Take my poor heart, and let it be
Forever closed to all but thee:
Seal thou my breast, and let me wear
That pledge of love forever there.

3 How blest are they who still abide
Close sheltered in thy bleeding side!
Who thence their life and strength derive,
And by thee move, and in thee live.

4 What are our works but sin and death,
Till thou thy quickening Spirit breathe?
Thou giv'st the power thy grace to move;
O wondrous grace! O wondrous love!

5 How can it be, thou heavenly King,
That thou shouldst us to glory bring?
Make slaves the partners of thy throne,
Decked with a never-fading crown?

6 Hence our hearts melt, our eyes o'erflow,
Our words are lost, nor will we know,
Nor will we think of aught beside,
"My Lord, my Love is crucified."
—NICOLAUS L. ZINZENDORF.

Crowning Jesus.

Arranged by R. Kelso Carter.

58   Lord of All.

1 Come, all ye saints, salute your King,
   At Jesus' feet now fall;
   A living sacrifice to bring,
   And crown him Lord of all.

Cho.—We'll crown him Lord of all,
   We'll crown him Lord of all:
   The Son of God, Eternal Word,
   We'll crown him Lord of all.

2 His light upon our souls hath gleamed,
   His mercies softly call,
   That we, by his own blood redeemed,
   Should crown him Lord of all.

3 On him all guilt and sin are laid,
   His grace and love enthrall;
   Himself our righteousness is made,
   Then crown him Lord of all.

4 No crown of thorns our love now brings
   In Pilate's judgment hall;
   On heaven's throne, O King of kings!
   We'll crown thee Lord of all.
                  —R. K. C.

Copyright, 1889, by R. Kelso Carter.

61   King of Kings.

1 A glad new song of peace and love
   My soul with rapture sings;
   I soon shall join the saints above,
   And crown him King of kings.

Cho.—We'll crown him King of kings,
   We'll crown him King of kings:
   In honor, majesty, and power,
   We'll crown him King of kings.

2 Before his feet I kneel to-day,
   My soul her treasure brings;
   I bow to Jesus' royal sway,
   And crown him King of kings.

3 My Lord! my Life! while ages roll
   Salvation's anthem rings;
   Within the temple of my soul
   I'll crown thee King of kings.

4 With ransomed saints in heaven's dome
   I'll soar on angels' wings;
   When seraphs shout the harvest home
   We'll crown him King of kings.
                  —R. K. C.

59   When I survey the wondrous cross.   Tune, Rockingham, p. 30.

1 When I survey the wondrous cross,
   On which the Prince of Glory died,
   My richest gain I count but loss,
   And pour contempt on all my pride.

2 Forbid it, Lord, that I should boast,
   Save in the death of Christ my God;
   All the vain things that charm me most,
   I sacrifice them to his blood.

3 See, from his head, his hands, his feet,
   Sorrow and love flow mingled down;
   Did e'er such love and sorrow meet?
   Or thorns compose so rich a crown?

4 Were the whole realm of nature mine,
   That were a present far too small;
   Love so amazing, so divine,
   Demands my soul, my life, my all.
                  —I. Watts

60   My body, soul, and spirit.   Key Eb.

1 My body, soul, and spirit,
   Jesus, I give to thee;
   A consecrated offering,
   Thine evermore to be.

Cho.—My all is on the altar,
   I'm waiting for the fire:
   Waiting, waiting, waiting,
   I'm waiting for the fire!

2 O Jesus mighty Saviour,
   I trust in thy great name;
   I look for thy salvation,
   Thy promise now I claim.

3 O let the fire descending
   Just now upon my soul,
   Consume my humble off'ring,
   And cleanse and make me whole.

4 I'm thine, O blessed Jesus,
   Washed by thy cleansing blood;
   Now seal me by thy Spirit,
   A sacrifice to God. —Mary D. James.

62. More Faith in Jesus.

Henrietta E. Blair.   Wm. J. Kirkpatrick.

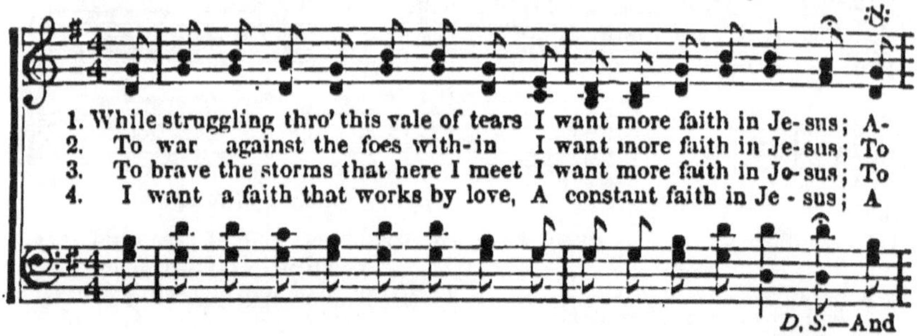

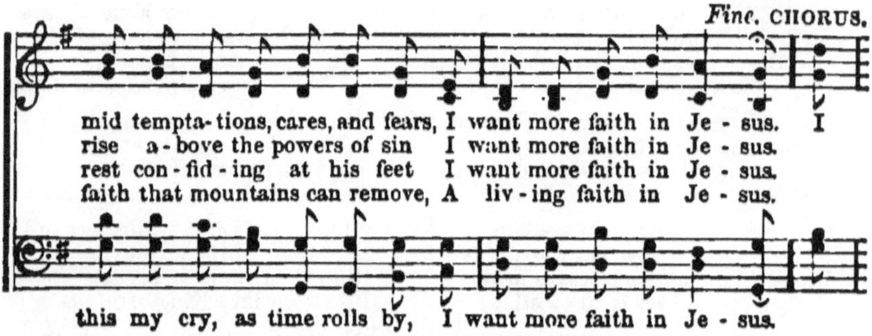

1. While struggling thro' this vale of tears I want more faith in Je-sus; A-
2. To war against the foes with-in I want more faith in Je-sus; To
3. To brave the storms that here I meet I want more faith in Je-sus; To
4. I want a faith that works by love, A constant faith in Je-sus; A

D. S.—And
Fine. CHORUS.

mid tempta-tions, cares, and fears, I want more faith in Je - sus. I
rise a-bove the powers of sin I want more faith in Je - sus.
rest con-fid-ing at his feet I want more faith in Je - sus.
faith that mountains can remove, A liv-ing faith in Je - sus.

this my cry, as time rolls by, I want more faith in Je - sus.

D. S.

want more faith, I want more faith, A clearer, brighter, stronger faith in Jesus;

Copyright, 1885, by John J. Hood.

63. Hallelujah! Amen.

Henrietta E. Blair.   Adapted and arr. by Wm. J. Kirkpatrick.

1. How oft in holy converse With Christ, my Lord, alone, I seem to hear the
2. They pass'd thro' toils and trials, And tho' the strife was long, They share the victor's
3. My soul takes up the chorus, And pressing on my way, Communing still with
4. Thro' grace I soon shall conquer, And reach my home on high; And thro' e-ternal

Hallelujah! Amen.—CONCLUDED.
CHORUS.

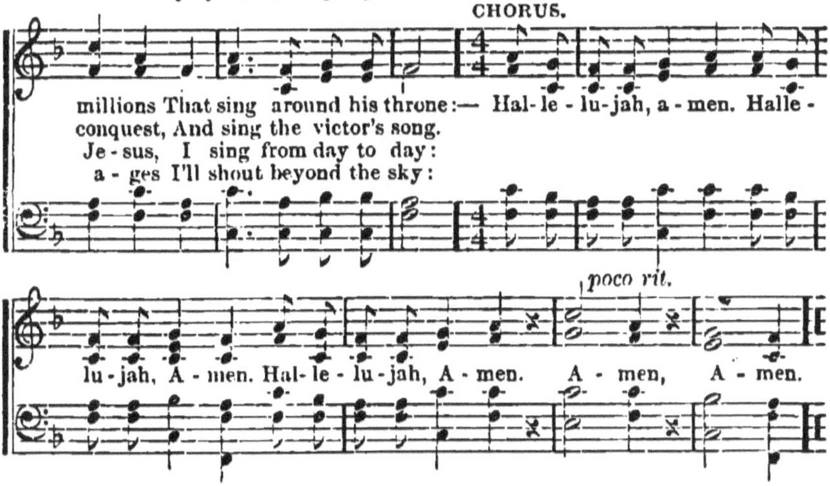

millions That sing around his throne:— Hal-le-lu-jah, a-men. Halle-
conquest, And sing the victor's song.
Je-sus, I sing from day to day:
a-ges I'll shout beyond the sky:

poco rit.

lu-jah, A-men. Hal-le-lu-jah, A-men. A-men, A-men.

64. The Joy of the Lord.
R. K. C.   R. Kelso Carter.

[whole:

1. Oh, the joy of the Lord, When with him in accord, By his power I'm ev'ry whit

by his power,

[1st. | 2d.

When my God doth impart His own peace to my heart,
And with rapture he blesses my soul, my soul.

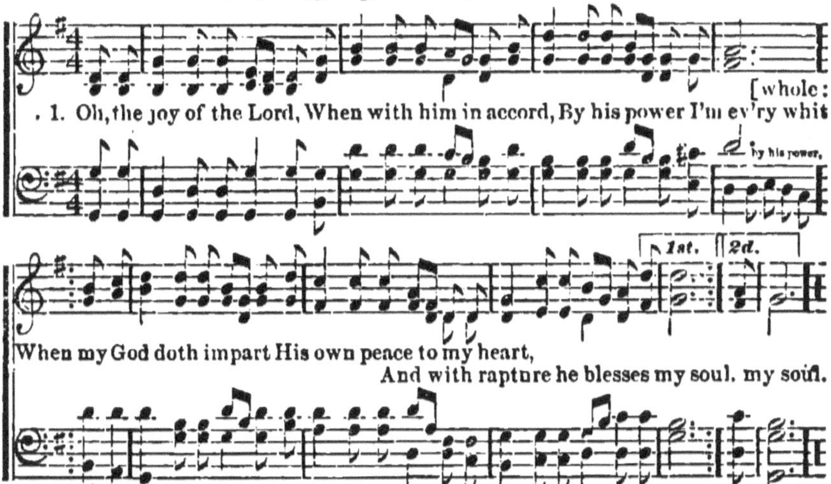

2 By the word of his might,
  To my eyes he gives sight
To behold wondrous things in his law;
  I shall never forget
  When he paid all my debt,
And his blood as a ransom I saw.

3 In my weakness I'm strong,
  I'm preserved from all wrong
And defended by God's mighty sword;
  Every foe he doth rout,
  I the victory do shout,
For my battles are fought by the Lord.

4 Through the dark clouds of sin,
  O'er the foes that within
Do beset me by day and by night;
  By my griefs and my graves—
  Over all Jesus saves,
Fills my soul with his own blessed light.

5 So I lift up my voice,
  And with angels rejoice
That my name is engraved on his palm:
  And I join with the throng
  Round the throne in the song,
I'm redeemed by the blood of the Lamb.

69. I Have a Blessed Hope To-day.

ADDIE MILLS. "Which hope we have as an anchor of the soul."—Heb. vi. 19. H. L. GILMOUR.

1. I have a bless-ed hope to-day, The gift thro' grace from Jesus came,
2. I have a live-ly hope within, And of the liv-ing One it sings
3. I have a hope that will a-bide, For faith and love support it well;

And while I walk the heavenly way I nev-er shall be put to shame;
Who cleanses now my heart from sin, And e'er to me good comfort brings;
The triple grace sprang from the tide Whose power the ransomed ever tell;

O bless-ed an-chor! hope divine! Se-cure I am while Christ is mine.
O bless-ed, liv-ing hope divine, I'll shout and sing while Christ is mine.
O blessed blood-bought hope divine! Praise Jesus, that such hope is mine.

Oh, hal-le-lu-jah! I can say, I have a bless-ed hope to-day.

4 I have a hope, let it abound;
O Holy Ghost, thy presence lend,
Make all my heart a fruitful ground.
Its lines forever let extend,
O blessed hope! O gift divine!
Thro' Christ its fulness now is mine.

5 I have a hope of glory bright,
A foretaste now of joys to come,
For Christ within, my Life and Light,
Assures me heaven is my home,
O blessed home where hope divine
Is lost in bliss, forever mine.

70. The Firm Foundation.

GEORGE KEITH. Tune, PORTUGUESE HYMN.

1. How firm a foundation, ye saints of the Lord, Is laid for your faith in his ex-cel-lent word! What more can he say, than to you he hath said, To you, who for re-fuge to Je-sus have fled?
2. "Fear not, I am with thee, O be not dismayed, For I am thy God, I will still give thee aid; cause thee to stand, Up-held by my gracious, om-ni-po-tent hand, Up-held by my gracious, om-ni-po-tent hand.
3. "When thro' the deep waters I call thee to go, The riv-ers of sor-row shall not o-ver-flow; For I will be with thee thy tri-als to bless, And sanc-ti-fy to thee thy deepest dis-tress, And sanc-ti-fy to thee thy deep-est dis-tress.
4. "When thro' fie-ry tri-als thy path-way shall lie, My grace all suf-fi-cient, shall be thy sup-ply, The flame shall not hurt thee; I on-ly de-sign Thy dross to consume, and thy gold to re-fine, Thy dross to consume, and thy gold to re-fine.

5 "E'en down to old age all my people shall prove [love;
My sovereign, eternal, unchangeable
And when hoary hairs shall their temples adorn, [be borne.
Like lambs they shall still in my bosom

6 "The soul that on Jesus hath leaned for repose,
I will not, I will not desert to his foes;
That soul, though all hell should endeavor to shake,
I'll never, no never, no never forsake!"

71. Can a Mother Forget?

F. G. Burroughs.   H. L. Gilmour.

1. Can a moth-er for-get the child of her love, The babe she hath nourished and blessed? Can she blot from her thoughts the flesh of her flesh, The in-fant she clasped to her breast?
2. Can a moth-er for-get the child of her prayers, The boy who her counsels may spurn? Though wandering now on the broad way of sin, She prays for the loved one's re-turn.
3. Can a moth-er for-get the child she has soothed When sobbing with ter-ror or grief? Will her heart, with its wealth of comfort, e'er fail To bring to her dar-ling re-lief!
4. Can a moth-er for-get? yea, ev-en she may Be deaf to the voice of thy plea; But He, whose compassions fail never, hath said, "My child, I will not for-get thee!"

CHORUS.

Can a moth-er for-get? can a moth-er for-get? Oh, sad is the answer, *she may:* But he who hath died for us will not for-get, Though far from his fold we may stray.

Copyright, 1889, by H. L. Gilmour.

4 My gladness, as on thee I wait,
  Can never half be told;
  The swelling joy seems most too great
  For human breast to hold.

5 My life is one long victor's shout,
  This earth's a lifeless clod;
  The gravitation's turned about,
  I'm going up to God.

73. And can it be?

CHARLES WESLEY. Arranged by WM. G. FISCHER.

1. { And can it be that I should gain An int'rest in the Saviour's blood?
   { Died he for me, who caused his pain? For me, who him to death pursued?
   D. C.—A-mazing love! how can it be, That thou, my Lord, should'st die for me?

2 'Tis myst'ry all: th' Immortal dies!
  Who can explore his strange design?
In vain the first-born seraph tries
  To sound the depths of love divine.
'Tis mercy all! let earth adore;
Let angel minds inquire no more.

3 He left his Father's throne above;
  (So free, so infinite his grace!)
Emptied himself of all but love,
  And bled for Adam's helpless race.
'Tis mercy all, immense and free,
For, O my God, it found out me!

4 Long my imprisoned spirit lay,
  Fast bound in sin and nature's night;
Thine eye diffused a quickening ray;
  I woke; the dungeon flamed with light;
My chains fell off, my heart was free—
I rose, went forth, and followed thee.

5 No condemnation now I dread;
  Jesus, with all in him, is mine;
Alive in him my living Head,
  And clothed in righteousness divine,
Bold I approach th' eternal throne,
And claim the crown thro' Christ my own.

---

74. Away, my unbelieving fear!

1 Away, my unbelieving fear!
   Fear shall in me no more have place;
My Saviour doth not yet appear—
   He hides the brightness of his face;
But shall I therefore let him go,
   And basely to the tempter yield?
No, in the strength of Jesus, no,
   I never will give up my shield.

2 Although the vine its fruit deny,
   Although the olive yield no oil,
The with'ring fig trees droop and die,
   The fields elude the tiller's toil:

The empty stall no herd afford,
   And perish all the bleating race;
Yet will I triumph in the Lord,
   The God of my salvation praise.

3 In hope, believing against hope,
   Jesus, my Lord, my God I claim;
Jesus, my strength, shall lift me up;
   Salvation is in Jesus' name:
To me he soon shall bring it nigh,
   My soul shall then outstrip the wind;
On wings of love mount up on high,
   And leave the world and sin behind.
—CHARLES WESLEY.

75. The Haven of Rest.

Dr. H. L. Gilmour.   Geo. D. Moore.

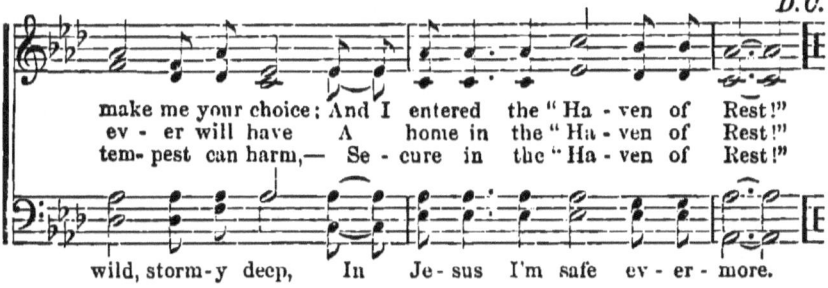

1. My soul, in sad exile, was out on life's sea, So burdened with sin, and distrest, Till I heard a sweet voice saying, Of Jesus, who'll save whosoever will have A home in the "Haven of Rest!"
2. The song of my soul, since the Lord made me whole, Has been the OLD STORY so blest Of Jesus, who'll save whosoever will have A home in the "Haven of Rest!"
3. How precious the thought that we all may recline, Like John the beloved and blest, On Jesus' strong arm, where no tempest can harm,— Secure in the "Haven of Rest!"

CHORUS.—I've anchored my soul in the haven of rest, I'll sail the wide seas no more; The tempest may sweep o'er the wild, stormy deep, In Jesus I'm safe evermore.

4 I yielded myself to his tender embrace,
And faith taking hold of the word,
My fetters fell off, and I anchored my [soul;
The haven of rest is my Lord.

5 Oh, come to the Saviour, he patiently waits
To save by his power divine;
Come, anchor your souls in the haven of [rest,
And say, "my Beloved is mine."

Mrs. E. H. Gates.   **Home of the Soul.**   Tune and chorus above.

1 I will sing you a song of that beautiful land,
The far away home of the soul,
Where no storms ever beat on the glittering strand,
While the years of eternity roll.

2 Oh, that home of the soul! in my visions and dreams
Its bright, jasper walls I can see;
Till I fancy but thinly the vail intervenes
Between the fair city and me.

3 That unchangable home is for you and for me,
Where Jesus of Nazareth stands;
The King of all kingdoms forever, is he,
And he holdeth our crowns in his hands.

4 Oh, how sweet it will be in that beautiful land,
So free from all sorrow and pain;
With songs on our lips and with harps in our hands
To meet one another again.

Copyright, 1889, by John J. Hood.

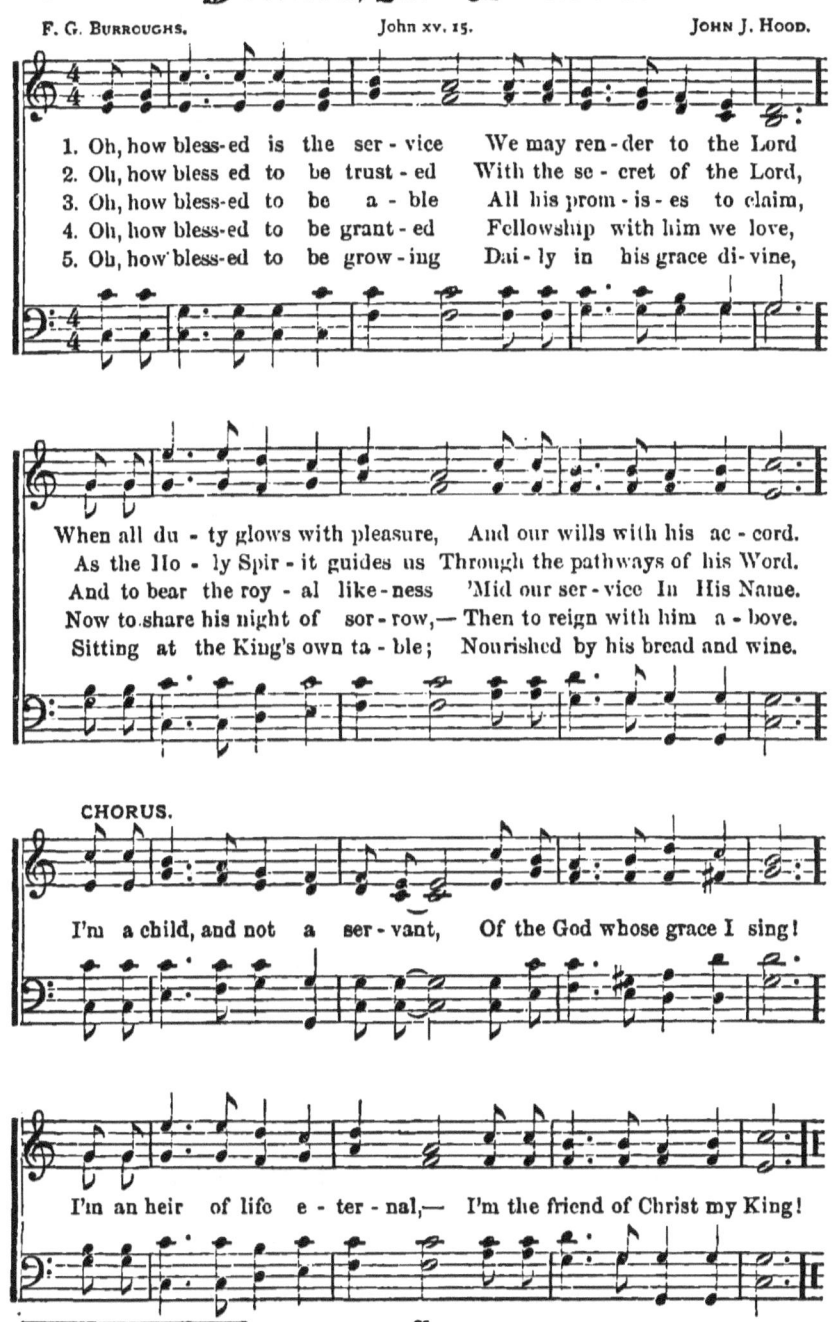

81. The Blood-Washed Pilgrim.

R. Kelso Carter.   Arranged.

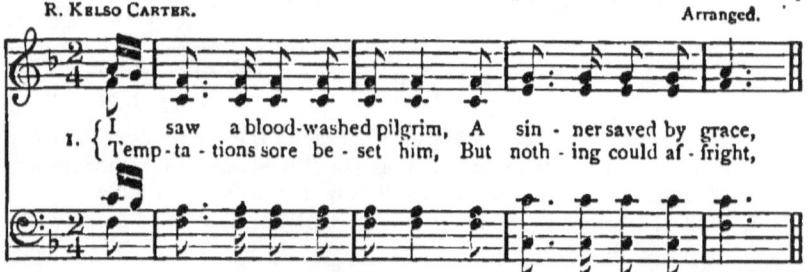

1. I saw a blood-washed pilgrim, A sin-ner saved by grace,
Upon the king's great highway, With peaceful, shining face.

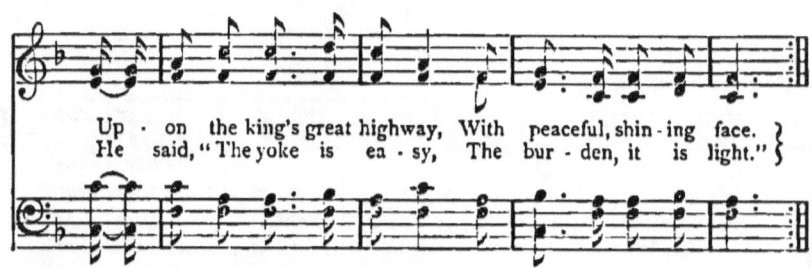

Temp-ta-tions sore beset him, But nothing could af-fright,
He said, "The yoke is ea-sy, The bur-den, it is light."

Chorus.

Oh! palms of vic-to-ry, crowns of glo-ry, Palms of vic-to-ry I shall wear.

2.
His helmet was Salvation,
  A simple Faith his shield,
And Righteousness his breast-plate;
  The Spirit's sword he'd wield.
All fiery darts arrested,
  And quenched their blazing flight;
He cried, "The yoke is easy,
  The burden, it is light."—Cho.

3.
I saw him in the furnace,
  He doubted not, nor feared,
And in the flames beside him
  The Son of God appeared.
Though seven times 'twas heated
  With all the tempter's might,
He said, "The yoke is easy,
  The burden, it is light."—Cho.

4.
Mid storms, and clouds, and trials,
  In prison, at the stake,
He leaped for joy, rejoicing,
  'Twas all for Jesus' sake.
That God should count him worthy,
  Was such supreme delight,
He cried, "The yoke is easy,
  The burden, is so light."—Cho.

5.
I saw him overcoming,
  Through all the swelling strife,
Until he crossed the threshold
  Of God's Eternal Life.
The Crown, the Throne, the Sceptre,
  The Name, the Stone so White,
Were his, who found, in Jesus,
  The yoke and burden light.—Cho.

Copyright, 1886, by R. K. Carter.

84. He that Overcometh.

R. K. C. — Rev. xii. 11. — R. Kelso Carter.

1. To him that o-ver-com-eth, To him that o-ver-com-eth
2. To him that o-ver-com-eth, To him that o-ver-com-eth
3. To him that o-ver-com-eth, To him that o-ver-com-eth

Will I give the tree of life, In the par-a-dise of God.
Will I give the hid-den manna, And the stone with the new, new name.
Will I give the power o'er the nations, And the Bright and Morning Star.

CHORUS.

O, we o-vercome by the blood, by the blood, And the vict'ry of our faith o'er the world:
By the blood, and the word of our testi-mony; Oh! praise ye the Lord!

4 To him that overcometh,
  To him that overcometh
  White raiment shall be given,
  And a name in the book of life.

5 Oh, he that overcometh,
  Oh, he that overcometh
  Shall be made a pillar in the temple,
  And he shall no more go out.

6 To him that overcometh,
  To him that overcometh
  Will I grant to sit in my throne,
  Even as I have overcome.

7 O, he that overcometh,
  All things he shall inherit:
  And I will be his God,
  And he shall be my son.

Copyright, 1886, by John J. Hood.

Arise, Shine.—CONCLUDED.

REFRAIN. *Faster.*

Rise, shine, for thy light is come,
Rise and shine, oh, rise and shine, for now thy light is come, is come, oh,

Rise, shine, for thy light is come;
Rise and shine, oh, rise and shine, for now thy light is come, is come;

And the glo-ry of the Lord is risen up-on thee:
And the glo-ry, and the glo-ry of the Lord is risen up-on thee:

rit.

Rise, shine, for thy light is come.
Rise and shine, oh, rise and shine, for now thy

5 The sun and the moon shall no longer be bright,
 The Lord everlasting shall shine as thy light:
 Thy people all righteous, his mercies adore,
 Inherit the land of the Lord evermore.

87. Jesus is Good to Me.

Rev. E. H. Stokes, D. D.   Jno. R. Sweney.

1. I love my Saviour, his heart is good, He has loved me o'er and o'er;
2. He calls, I rise, and he maketh me whole,—How fond his tender embrace!
3. I want to love him with all my heart, Tho' all its powers are small;
4. He's good to me in my sorrow's night, He's good in the tempest's roll;

He sought me wand'ring, I'm saved by his blood, And I love him more and more.
He cleanses and keeps me and blesses my soul,—My day the smile of his face.
I will not keep from him any part, For he is worthy of all.
He bringeth from darkness into light,—With joy he filleth my soul.

CHORUS.

Je - sus is good to me, . . . Je - sus is good to me; . . .
          to me,   to me;

So good! so good! Je - sus is good to my soul.

92. Blessed be the Name.

W. H. CLARK. Arranged by WM. J. KIRKPATRICK.

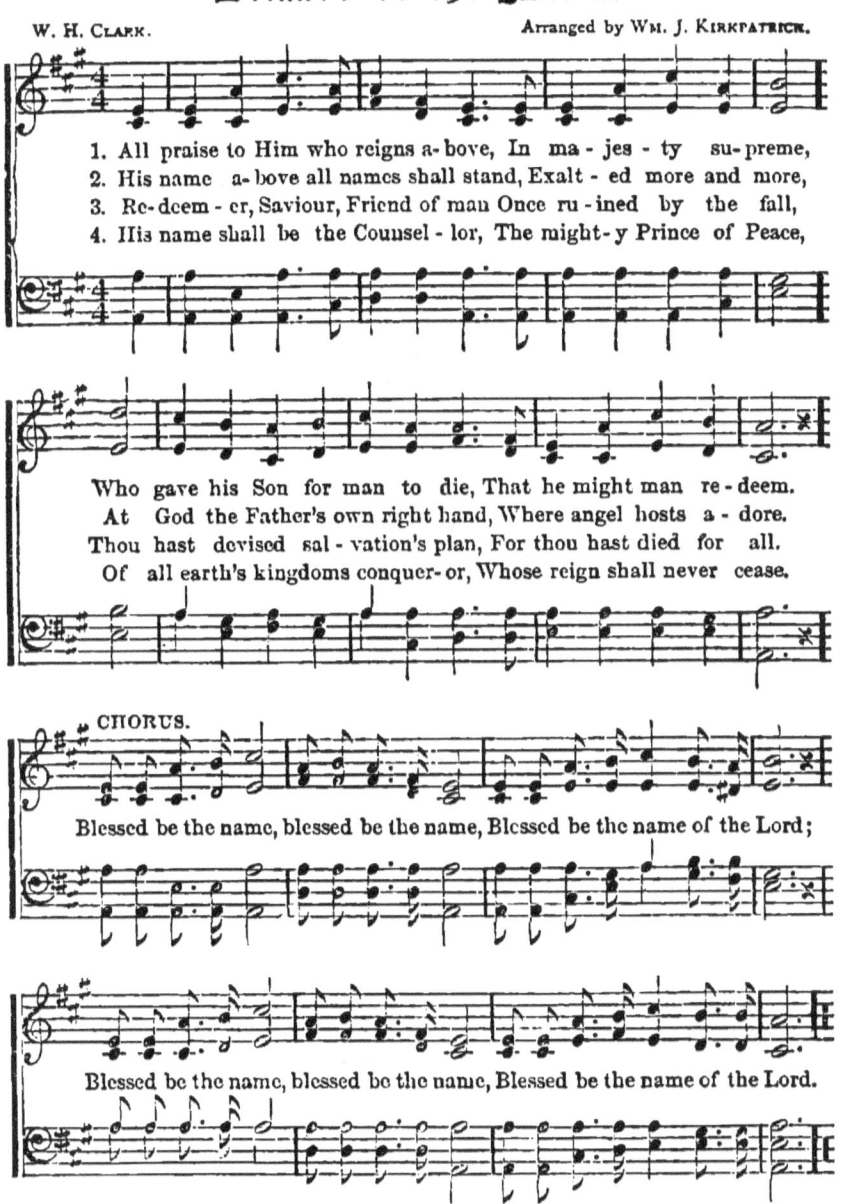

1. All praise to Him who reigns a-bove, In ma-jes-ty su-preme,
2. His name a-bove all names shall stand, Exalt-ed more and more,
3. Re-deem-er, Saviour, Friend of man Once ru-ined by the fall,
4. His name shall be the Counsel-lor, The might-y Prince of Peace,

Who gave his Son for man to die, That he might man re-deem.
At God the Father's own right hand, Where angel hosts a-dore.
Thou hast devised sal-vation's plan, For thou hast died for all.
Of all earth's kingdoms conquer-or, Whose reign shall never cease.

CHORUS.

Blessed be the name, blessed be the name, Blessed be the name of the Lord;

Blessed be the name, blessed be the name, Blessed be the name of the Lord.

5 The ransomed hosts to thee shall bring
  Their praise and homage meet;
  With rapturous awe adore their King,
  And worship at his feet.

6 Then shall we know as we are known,
  And in that world above
  Forever sing around the throne
  His everlasting love.

Copyright, 1888, by WM J. KIRKPATRICK

93. I Love Thee, my Saviour.

Dedicated to the Friends, Portsmouth, R. I.

R. K. C. — R. Kelso Carter.

1. I love Thee, my Saviour, Thy touch makes me whole;
   I'll praise Thee for-ev-er For sav-ing my soul.
2. I love Thee, my Saviour, For, when lost in sin,
   Thou sought me and found me, Thy blood made me clean.
3. I love Thee, my Saviour, When tempt-ed and tried,
   My pre-cious Re-deem-er Walks close by my side.

Cho. — To Christ, my Re-deem-er, Who sav-eth my soul.
Hal-le-lu-jah! Hal-le-lu-jah! Let the glad prais-es roll.

4 I love Thee, my Saviour,
Though dark grows the night;
While watching for Jesus,
I walk in the light.

5 I love Thee, my Saviour,
O Lord, quickly come,
With saints in Thy glory
To welcome us home.

Copyright, 1888, by R. K. Carter.

94.

Tune—"What a Friend we have in Jesus."   Key F.

1 What a friend we have in Jesus,
  All our sins and griefs to bear;
What a privilege to carry
  Ev'ry thing to God in prayer.
Oh, what peace we often forfeit,
  Oh, what needless pain we bear—
All because we do not carry
  Ev'ry thing to God in prayer.

2 Have we trials and temptations?
  Is there trouble anywhere?
We should never be discouraged,
  Take it to the Lord in prayer.
Can we find a Friend so faithful,
  Who will all our sorrows share?
Jesus knows our every weakness,
  Take it to the Lord in prayer.

3 Are we weak and heavy laden,
  Cumbered with a load of care?
Precious Saviour, still our refuge,—
  Take it to the Lord in prayer;
Do thy friends despise, forsake thee?
  Take it to the Lord in prayer.
In His arms He'll take and shield thee
  Thou wilt find a solace there.

95. In His Kingdom.

Dedicated to the Society of Christian Endeavor.

B. K. C.
R. KELSO CARTER.

1. I will sing of a time, of a land, and a King, Drawing nigh to the souls of the blest; Where the weary and worn, from all sorrow and care, In His kingdom eternally rest.
2. I will sing of a conflict, a victory won, Of a flag that shall never go down; Where no sin ever comes, and for soldiers of Christ, In His kingdom is laid up a crown.
3. I will sing of the dear ones who've left us and gone To reunion at headquarters above; Of a time when we'll gather again to our hearts, In His kingdom, once more, those we love.
4. I will sing of a Saviour who died for my soul, And bought me with blood's ebbing tide; In the mansions prepared by the river of life, In His kingdom, with Him I'll abide.

CHORUS.

There'll be rest for the weary, Vict'ry o-ver sin. Reunion with our lov'd ones, I can hardly take it in; A-wake in Jesus' likeness, I shall be satisfied; And I'll swell the hallelujahs in His kingdom.

Copyright, 1889, by R. K. Carter.

96. Sing all the Way to Zion.

ABBIE MILLS. "The ransomed of the Lord shall come to Zion with songs." H. L. GILMOUR.

1. Sing all the way to Zi - on, For God is a - ble here
2. Sing of the power and glo - ry The weak - est saint may know,
3. Sing while in work a - bound - ing, Such as you find to do,
4. Sing soft - ly in the still - ness, When called a - part to rest,

To give you grace suf - fi - cient To ban - ish all your fear.
For Christ his strength has prom - ised Suf - fi - cient he'll be - stow
In an - y lot, wher - ev - er His wis - dom plac - es you;
And if the fur - nace glow - ing He sees for you is best,

T'ward you his grace a - bound - ing Through all your earth - ly days.
To make us al - ways tri - umph,—Yes, al - ways, saith his word,—
The song he gives in dark - ness May bring God's bless - ed light
His pres - ence there will wak - en A song that ne'er shall end,

Can you do less than ren - der A cease - less song of praise?
No foe can ev - er harm us While trust - ing in the Lord.
To some poor, lone - ly wan - d'rer, A - mid sin's gloomy night.
But loud - er growing, clear - er, With an - gel harps 'twill blend.

Copyright, 1889, by H. L. GILMOUR.

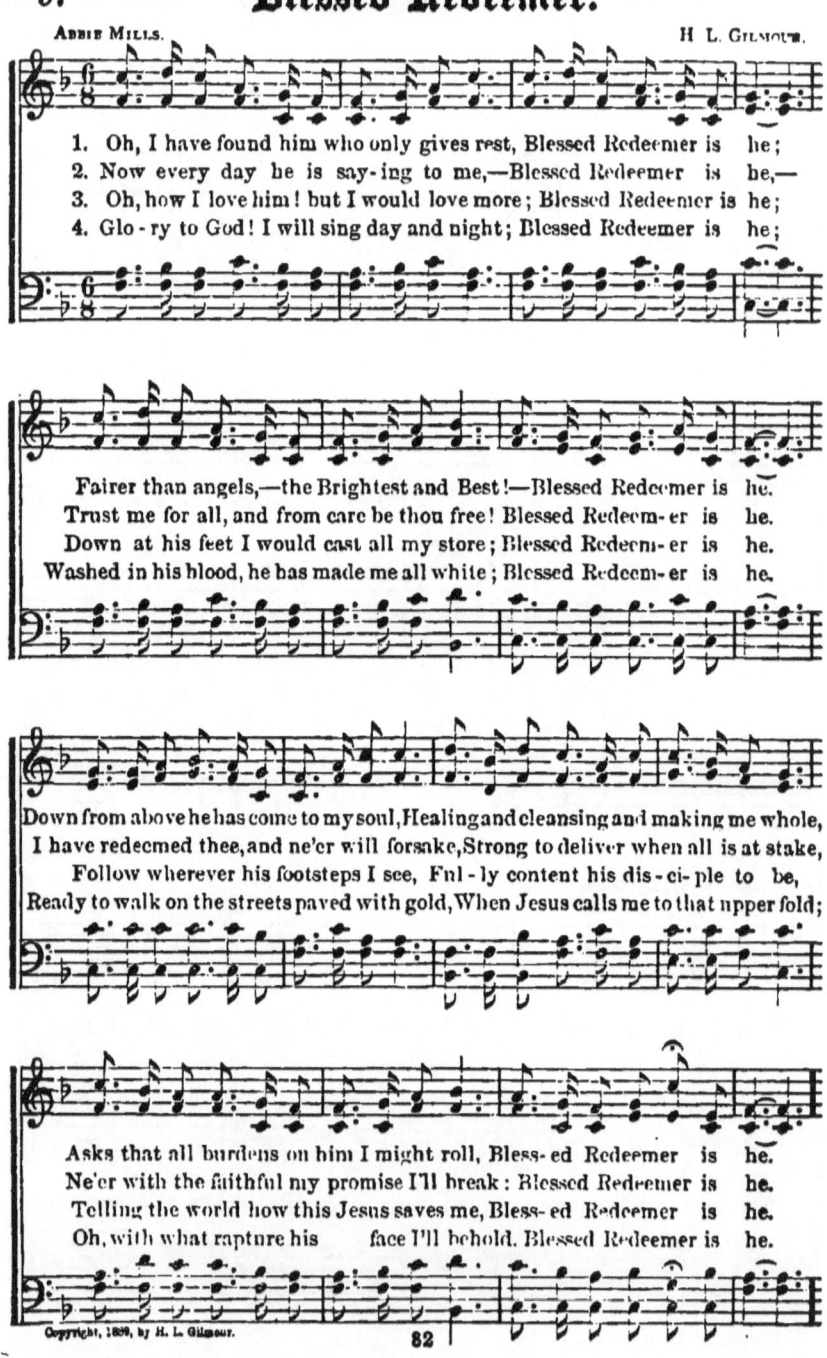

Blessed Redeemer.—CONCLUDED.

98. The Bridegroom Cometh!

R. K. C.   Plantation Melody, arranged by R. Kelso Carter.

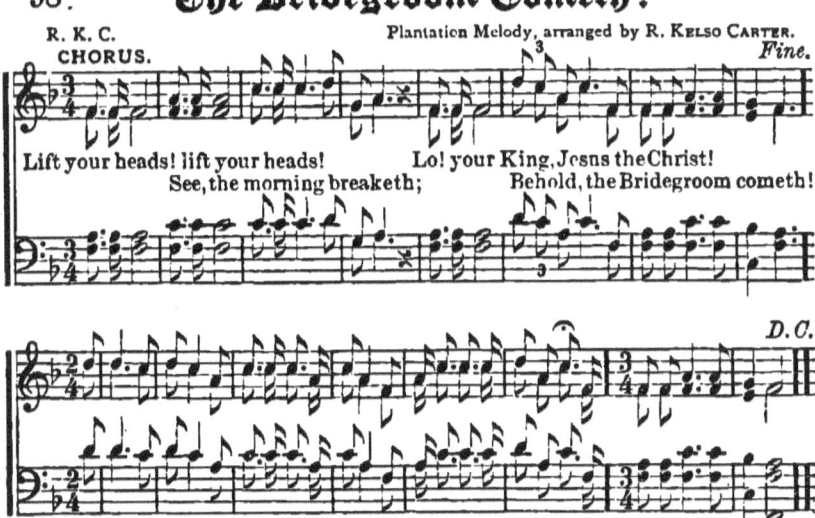

1 My Lord hath called me
  To meet him in the kingdom;
  The trumpet sounds it in my soul,
  Behold, the Bridegroom cometh!

2 The light is breaking,
  I see the rising splendor;
  The trumpet sounds it in my soul,
  Behold, the Bridegroom cometh!

3 I hear the music,
  From heavenly choirs ringing;
  The trumpet sounds it in my soul,
  Behold, the Bridegroom cometh!

4 Behold, he cometh!
  Oh, go ye forth to meet him!
  The trumpet sounds it in my soul,
  Behold, the Bridegroom cometh!

Copyright, 1889, by R. Kelso Carter.

99. Happy Day.

P. DODDRIDGE. English Melody.

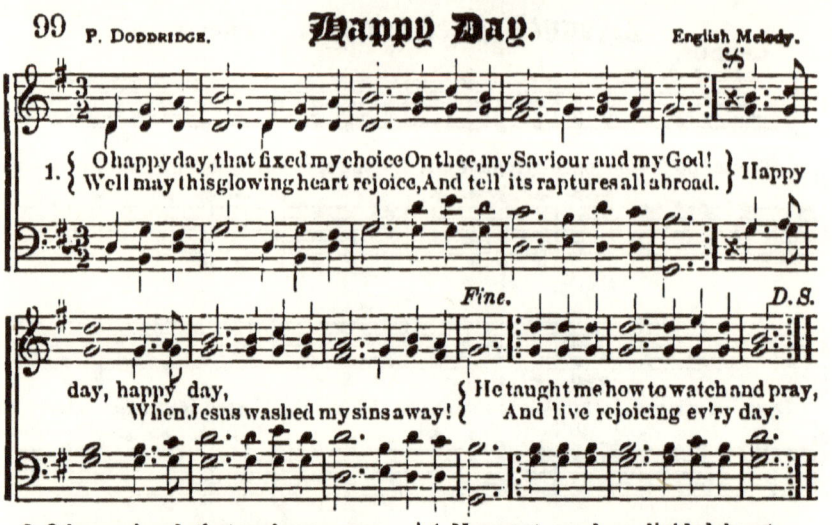

1. O happy day, that fixed my choice On thee, my Saviour and my God!
   Well may this glowing heart rejoice, And tell its raptures all abroad.
   Happy day, happy day, When Jesus washed my sins away!
   He taught me how to watch and pray, And live rejoicing ev'ry day.

2. O happy bond, that seals my vows
   To him who merits all my love!
   Let cheerful anthems fill his house,
   While to that sacred shrine I move.

3. 'Tis done! the great transaction's done!
   I am my Lord's, and he is mine:
   He drew me, and I followed on,
   Charmed to confess that voice divine.

4. Now rest, my long-divided heart;
   Fixed on this blissful center, rest;
   Nor ever from thy Lord depart;
   With him of every good possessed.

5. High heav'n that heard the solemn vow,
   That vow renewed shall daily hear,
   Till in life's latest hour I bow,
   And bless in death a bond so dear.

100. He Came to Save Me.

H. E. BLAIR. WM. J. KIRKPATRICK.

1. When Jesus laid his crown aside, He came to save me;
   When on the cross he bled and died, ... He came to save me.

2. In my poor heart he deigns to dwell, He came to save me;
   Oh, praise his name, I know it well, ... He came to save me.

REFRAIN.
I'm so glad, I'm so glad, I'm so glad that Jesus came, And grace is free,
He . . . came to save me.

3. With gentle hand he leads me still,
   He came to save me;
   And trusting him I fear no ill,
   He came to save me.

4. To him my faith with rapture clings,
   He came to save me;
   To him my heart looks up and sings,
   He came to save me.

Copyright, 1885, by WM. J. KIRKPATRICK.

101. Salvation's River.

R. Kelso Carter.   S. C. Foster.

1. { Down at the cross, on Calvary's mountain, Where mer-cies flow,
   { When nothing in the whole cre-a-tion Could purchase peace,
   I plunged in the redeem-ing fountain, Washed whiter than the snow. }
   My Saviour brought his free salva-tion, Gave me complete re-lease. }

CHORUS.
Broth-ers, wont you hear the sto-ry? See the fount-ain flow!
Oh, glo-ry in the highest, glo-ry! Je-sus saves me, this I know.

2 When lost in sin, my all I squandered,
   Far from the fold:
My Saviour sought me where I wandered,
   Gave me his wealth untold.
All bonds of sin and Satan rending,
   Christ made me whole:
I'll ne'er forget that joy transcending,
   When Jesus saved my soul.

3 All round my way the sun is shining,
   Darkness has fled:
On Jesus' breast I am reclining,
   Daily by him I'm fed.
My Lord has cast his robe around me,
   No more I'll roam;
The Shepherd of the sheep has found me,
   Jesus has brought me home.

Copyright, 1889, by R. Kelso Carter.   Melody by per. O. Ditson Co., owners of copyright.

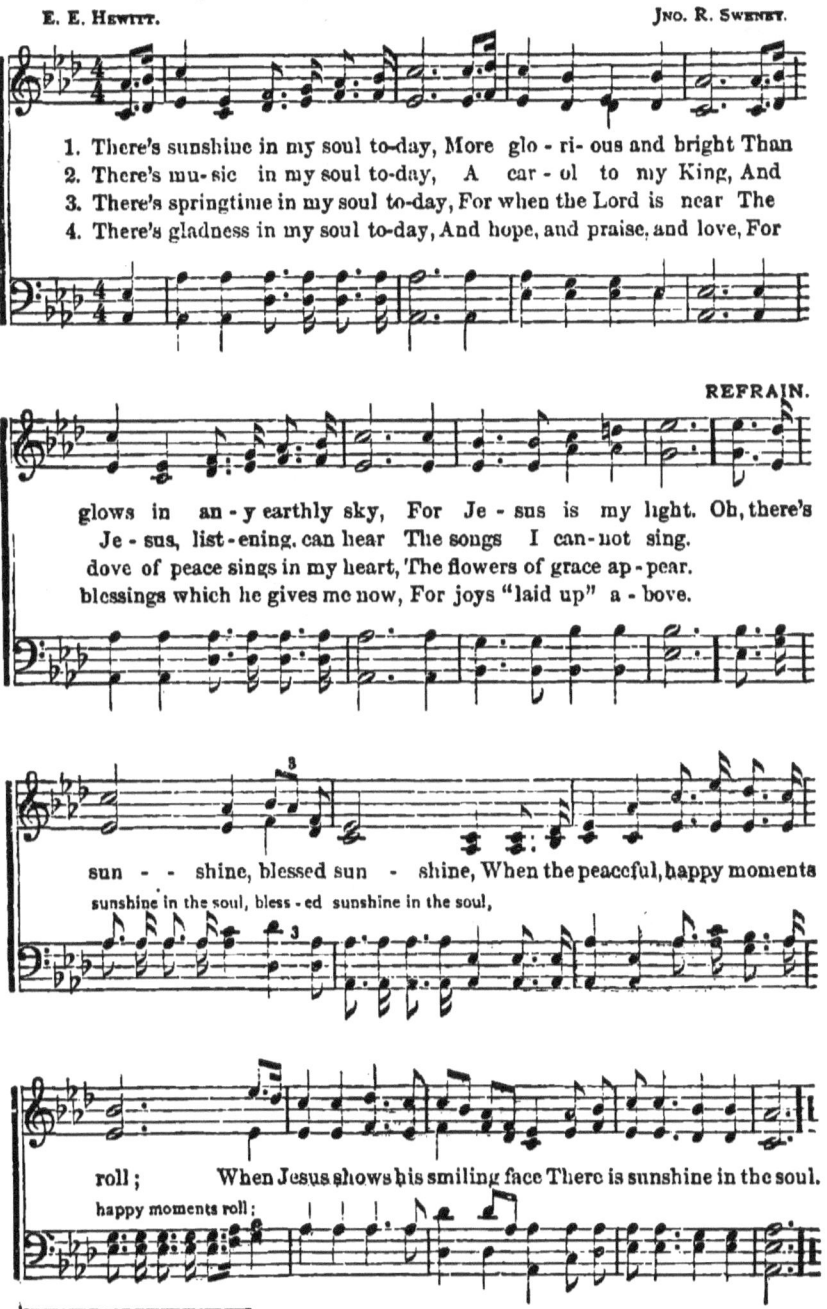

105. Washed in the Blood of the Lamb.

R. K. C.   R. Kelso Carter.

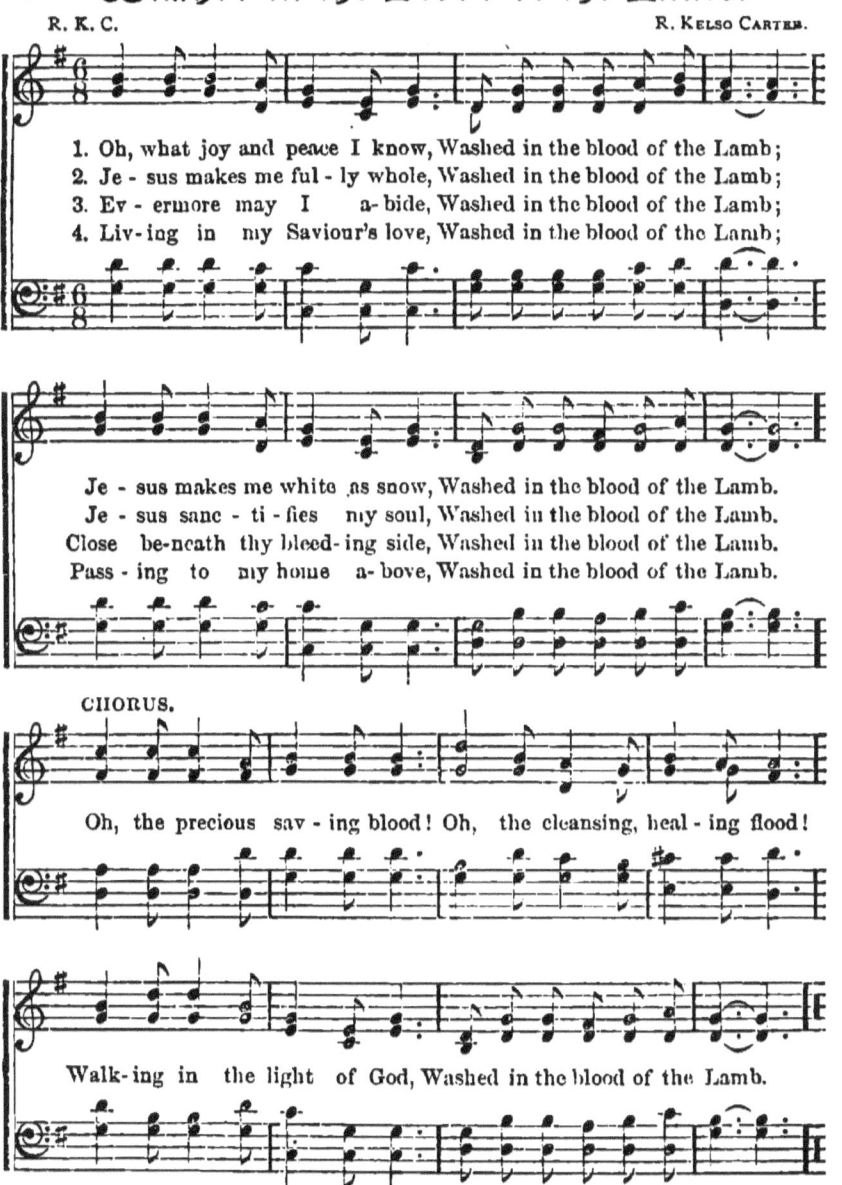

1. Oh, what joy and peace I know, Washed in the blood of the Lamb;
2. Je - sus makes me ful - ly whole, Washed in the blood of the Lamb;
3. Ev - ermore may I a - bide, Washed in the blood of the Lamb;
4. Liv - ing in my Saviour's love, Washed in the blood of the Lamb;

Je - sus makes me white as snow, Washed in the blood of the Lamb.
Je - sus sanc - ti - fies my soul, Washed in the blood of the Lamb.
Close be - neath thy bleed - ing side, Washed in the blood of the Lamb.
Pass - ing to my home a - bove, Washed in the blood of the Lamb.

CHORUS.

Oh, the precious sav - ing blood! Oh, the cleansing, heal - ing flood!

Walk - ing in the light of God, Washed in the blood of the Lamb.

5 Now by faith we overcome,
   Washed in the blood of the Lamb;
   Hear, ye deaf, and shout, ye dumb,
   Washed in the blood of the Lamb.

6 Knowing him, and him alone,
   Washed in the blood of the Lamb;
   Soon we'll meet around the throne,
   Washed in the blood of the Lamb.

Copyright, 1886, by John J. Hood.

107. I'm more than Conqueror.

PARKER. R. KELSO CARTER.

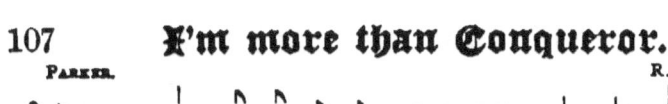

1. I'm more than conq'ror thro' his blood, Je-sus saves me now; I
2. Be-fore the bat-tle lines are spread, Je-sus saves me now; Be-
3. I'll ask no more that I may see, Je-sus saves me now; His
4. Why should I ask a sign from God? Je-sus saves me now; Can

rest beneath the shield of God, Je-sus saves me now. I go a
fore the boasting foe is dead, Je-sus saves me now. I win the
prom-ise is enough for me, Je-sus saves me now. Though foes be
I not trust the precious blood? Je-sus saves me now. Strong in his

kingdom to ob-tain, I shall thro' him the vict'ry gain,—Je-sus
fight tho' not be-gun, I'll trust and shout, still marching on,—Je-sus
strong and walls be high, I'll shout, he gives the vic-to-ry,— Je-sus
word, I meet the foe, And, shouting, win without a blow,— Je-sus

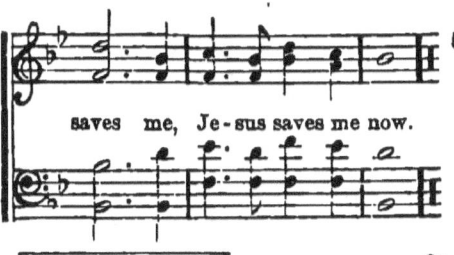

saves me, Je-sus saves me now.

5 Should Satan come like 'whelming [waves,
Jesus saves me now;
Ere trials crush my Father saves,
Jesus saves me now.
He hides me till the storm is past,
For me he tempers every blast,—
Jesus saves me now.

Copyright, 1886, by JOHN J. HOOD.

108 What Wondrous Love is This.

Altered and enlarged by R. K. C. Arranged by R. Kelso Carter.

5 And when to Jordan's flood
We have come, O my soul!
And when to Jordan's flood
We have come;
Jehovah rules the tide,
The water he'll divide,
And welcome home his Bride,
Praise the Lord, O my soul!
And welcome home his Bride,
O my soul!

[*Additional verses on opposite page.*]

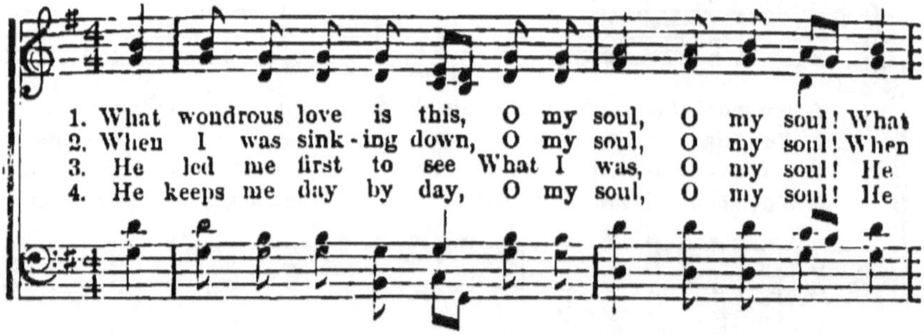

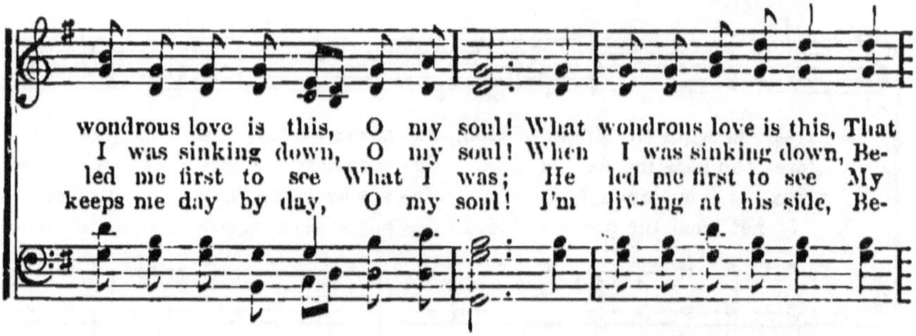

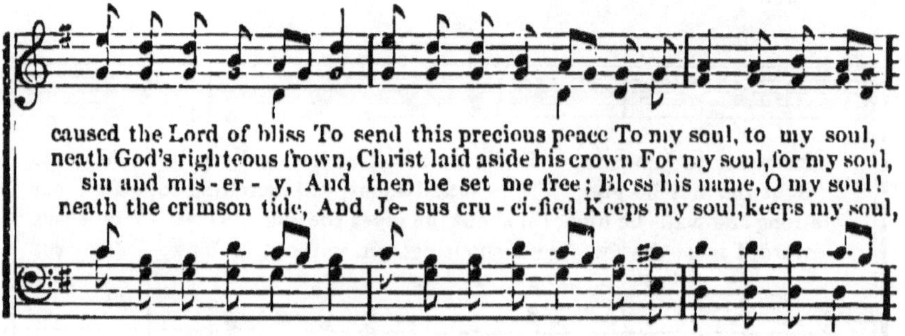

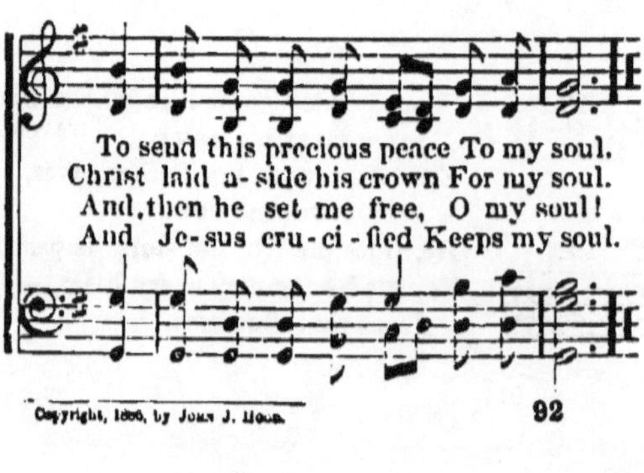

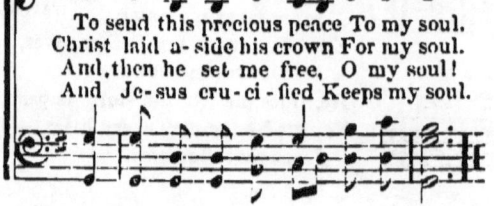

109

Rev. WM. HUNTER, D. D. Arr. by T. C. O'KANE.

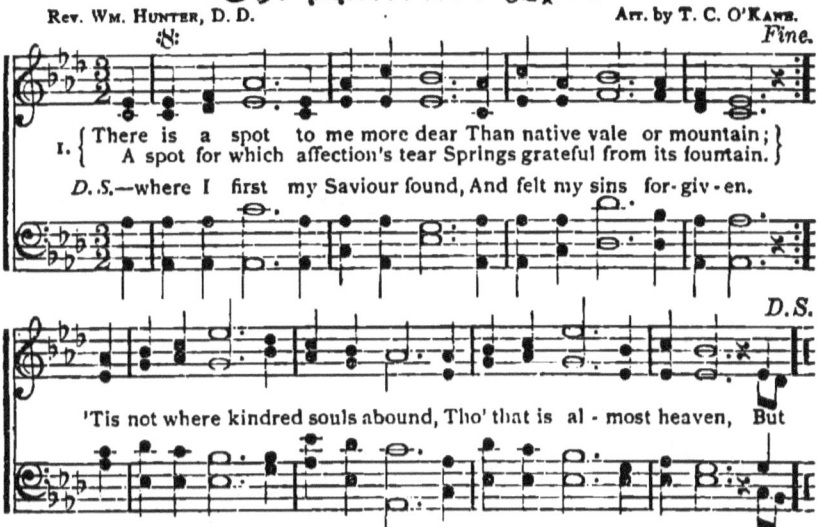

1. There is a spot to me more dear Than native vale or mountain;
   A spot for which affection's tear Springs grateful from its fountain.

D. S.—where I first my Saviour found, And felt my sins for-giv-en.

'Tis not where kindred souls abound, Tho' that is al-most heaven, But

2 Hard was my toil to reach the shore,
  Long tossed upon the ocean:
  Above me was the thunder's roar,
  Beneath the waves' commotion.
  Darkly the pall of night was thrown
  Around me, faint with terror;
  In that dark hour how did my groan
  Ascend for years of error.

3 Sinking and panting as for breath
  I knew not help was near me;
  I cried, "Oh, save me, Lord, from death,
  Immortal Jesus, hear me;

  Then quick as thought I felt him mine.
  My Saviour stood before me;
  I saw his brightness round me shine,
  And shouted "Glory, glory."

4 O sacred hour! O hallowed spot!
  Where love divine first found me;
  Wherever falls my distant lot
  My heart shall linger round thee.
  And when from earth I rise, to soar
  Up to my home in heaven,
  Down will I cast my eyes once more,
  Where I was first forgiven.

---

110 Amid a world of sin. Tune, "Wondrous Love,"
opposite page.

1 AMID a world of sin,
    O my soul, O my soul!:‖
  Beset on every hand
  Against the foe I stand,
  Yet seek a better land,
    Praise the Lord, O my soul!
  Yet seek a better land,
    O my soul!

2 I'm weary oftentimes,
    O my soul, O my soul!:‖
  But, spite of every fear,
  I read my title clear;
  The kingdom draweth near,
    Praise the Lord, etc.

3 Behold the Bridegroom comes,
    O my soul, O my soul!:‖

  Then sound the midnight cry;
  Look up, who weary sigh!
  The King of kings is nigh,
    Praise the Lord, etc.

4 He's coming back again,
    O my soul, O my soul!:‖
  He's coming back again,
  No more a Saviour slain,
  A King, he comes to reign,
    Praise the Lord, etc.

5 He comes to right all wrong,
    O my soul, O my soul!:‖
  With trump and victor's song,
  With saints ten thousand strong,
  It won't be very long,
    Praise the Lord, etc.   —R. K. C.

Missing.

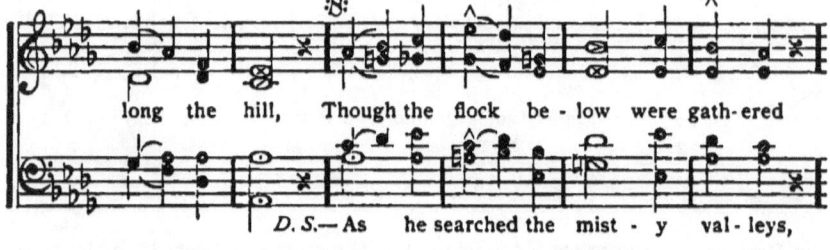

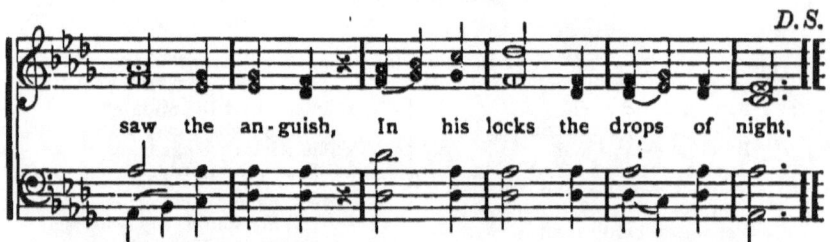

2 Just one tender lamb was missing,
 When he called them all by name;
 While the others heard and followed
 This one, only, never came.
 Oft his voice rang thro' the darkness
 Of that long, long night of pain,
 Oft he vainly paused to listen
 For an answering tone again.

3 Far away the truant sleeping,
 By the chasm of despair;
 Lay unconscious of its danger,
 Shivering in the mountain air.
 But at last the Shepherd found it,
 Found it ere in sleep it died,
 Took it in his loving bosom,
 And his soul was satisfied.

Copyright, 1882, by H. L. Gilmour.

113. For Jesus' Sake.

EUGENIE of Sweden was ordered by her physician to go to an island off the coast for her health. Finding there sick and helpless cripples, she conceived the idea of building and endowing a hospital for them; but how to get the means she knew not. At last she wrote her brother, asking permission to sell her family jewels "*for Christ's sake;*" and on the strength of this plea he consented, and the hospital was built. One day the Princess, who was a ministering angel in the hospital her self-sacrifice had bought, was sitting by the side of a dying woman, when with her last strength she raised herself in bed to caress the hand of her benefactor, and fell back dead. Eugenie looked down at her hand, saw the grateful tears glistening on it in the sunlight, and lifting her eyes to God, exclaimed, "*O my Saviour, I sold my jewels for thee, but thou hast restored them, and oh, how much more beautiful!*" Such transformation awaits all sacrifices *for Jesus' sake.*

ABBIE MILLS.   H. L. GILMOUR.

1. For Jesus' sake I sold my all, And laid the price at his dear feet; It was an off-'ring, oh, so small! But his peculiar smile how sweet! On errands for my King I sped, Upborne by wings of love divine, The weariness of life had fled, His rest, and peace, and joy were mine.
2. The dying blest me as I told Of wondrous love, of heaven and home, Bought with a price above fine gold, From which they nevermore should roam. My ornaments, the glitt'ring tear, On hands bestowed once decked with gems; In heaven's light, lo! these appear More brilliant than earth's diadems.
3. O precious Saviour, then I cried, I gave my jewels up for thee; The kiss of love the want supplied, And left these beauteous pearls for me. And when all tears are wiped away, The halo shall the brighter flame Thro' all the glad, eternal day, Around all marked, "In Jesus' name."

Copyright, 1899, by H. L. Gilmour.

For Jesus' Sake.—CONCLUDED.

CHORUS.

O Jesus, Jesus, more to me Than all my heart once held so dear, What beauty I behold in thee, What bliss to feel thee ever near!

114. O Thou in whose. Tune, MEDITATION. 11,8.

JOSEPH SWAIN.   FREEMAN LEWIS, arr. by HUBERT P. MAIN.

1. O thou in whose presence my soul takes delight,
On whom in affliction I call,
My comfort by day and my song in the night,
My hope, my salvation, my all!

2. Where dost thou, dear Shepherd, resort with thy sheep,
To feed them in pastures of love?
Say, why in the valley of death should I weep,
Or alone in this wilderness rove?

3. Or why should I wander an alien from thee,
Or cry in the desert for bread?
Thy foes will rejoice when my sorrows they see,
And smile at the tears I have shed.

4. Ye daughters of Zion, declare, have you seen
The star that on Israel shone?
Say if in your tents my Beloved has been,
And where with his flocks he has gone.

5. He looks! and ten thousands of angels rejoice,
And myriads wait for his word;
He speaks! and eternity, filled with his voice,
Re-echoes the praise of the Lord.

6. Dear Shepherd, I hear, and will follow thy call;
I know the sweet sound of thy voice;
Restore and defend me, for thou art my all,
And in thee I will ever rejoice.

The Silver Trumpet-G

116. I Praise the Lord.

H. L. G. — Dr. H. L. Gilmour.
Har. by Mame P. Gilmour.

1. I praise the Lord, when full of sin A willing Saviour took me in,
2. I praise the Lord, when I was blind, And knew not where the path to find,
3. I praise the Lord I'm in the way, My prospect bright'ning ev'ry day,

And now I love to dwell with him; Oh, glo-ry, hal-le-lu-jah!
The Spir-it came, with words so kind, And pointed me to Je-sus.
And, Je-sus help-ing, I will stay, And nev-er leave my Sav-iour.

CHORUS.

Glo-ry, glo-ry to his name; Hal-le-lu-jah, Je-sus came; I praise the Lord the Lamb was slain To save a world of sin-ners.

4 I praise the Lord, I follow on,
  Obedient to the heavenly call;
  I rest in Christ, my all in all,
  A perfect, loving Saviour.
5 I praise the Lord, 'mid raging storm
  My soul has refuge from alarm
  By resting on the mighty arm
  Of Jesus Christ my Saviour.

6 I praise the Lord for sweet repose
  From inward fears and outward foes;
  A peaceful stream of pleasure flows
  When leaning on my Saviour.
7 I praise the Lord for peace within;
  I praise the Lord I'm cleansed from sin;
  I praise the Lord I'm free in him;
  Oh, glory, hallelujah!

Copyright, 1887, by John J. Hood.

117 Jesus Comes.

Mrs. Phœbe Palmer. Wm. J. Kirkpatrick.

1. Watch, ye saints, with eyelids waking, Lo, the pow'rs of heav'n are shaking,
2. Lo! the promise of your Saviour, Pardoned sin and purchased favor,
3. Kingdoms at their base are crumbling, Hark, his chariot wheels are rumbling,
4. Nations wane, tho' proud and stately, Christ his kingdom hasteneth greatly,

Keep your lamps all trimm'd and burning, Ready for your Lord's return-ing.
Blood-wash'd robes and crowns of glory; Haste to tell redemption's sto - ry.
Tell, O, tell of grace abound- ing, Whilst the seventh trump is sounding.
Earth her latest pangs is summing, Shout, ye saints, your Lord is coming.

REFRAIN.

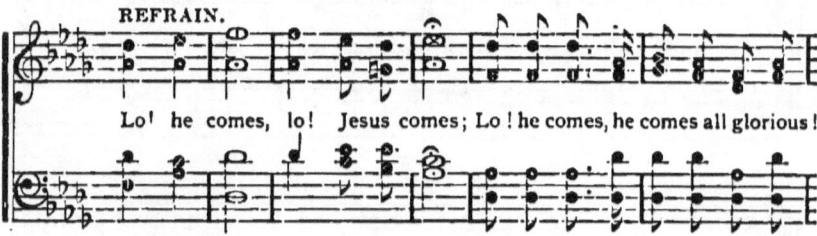

Lo! he comes, lo! Jesus comes; Lo! he comes, he comes all glorious!

Je-sus comes to reign victo-rious, Lo! he comes, yes, Je-sus comes.

5 Lamb of God!—thou meek and lowly,
  Judah's Lion!—high and holy,
  Lo! thy Bride comes forth to meet thee,
  All in blood-washed robes to greet thee,

6 Sinners, come, while Christ is pleading,
  Now for you he's interceding;
  Haste, ere grace and time diminished
  Shall proclaim the mystery finished.

Copyright, 1882, by Wm. J. Kirkpatrick.

122. It is Well with My Soul.

H. G. Spafford.   "He hath delivered my soul in peace."—Ps. lv. 18.   P. P. Bliss.

1. When peace, like a riv-er, at-tend-eth my way, When sorrows, like sea-bil-lows, roll; What-ev-er my lot, thou hast taught me to say, It is well, it is well with my soul. It is well ....
2. Though Satan should buffet, though trials should come, Let this blest as-sur-ance con-trol, That Christ hath re-gard-ed my help-less es-tate, And hath shed his own blood for my soul.
3. My sin—oh, the bliss of this glo-rious thought—My sin—not in part, but the whole, Is nailed to his cross and I bear it no more, Praise the Lord, praise the Lord, oh, my soul!
4. And, Lord, haste the day when the faith shall be sight, Tho clouds be rolled back as a scroll, The trump shall resound, and the Lord shall de-scend, "Ev-en so"—it is well with my soul.

CHORUS.

It is ...... with my soul, ... It is well, it is well with my soul.
well   with my soul,

124. Unsearchable Riches.

F. J. C. J. R. S.

1. O the unsearcha-ble rich-es of Christ!—Wealth that can never be told;—
2. O the unsearcha-ble rich-es of Christ, Who shall their greatness declare!
3. O the unsearcha-ble rich-es of Christ, Freely, how freely they flow;
4. O the unsearcha-ble rich-es of Christ! Who would not gladly endure

Riches exhaustless of mer-cy and grace, Precious, more precious than gold!
Jewels whose lustre our lives may a-dorn, Pearls that the poorest may wear.
Making the souls of the faithful and true Hap-py wherev-er they go.
Trials, afflictions, and crosses on earth, Riches like these to se-cure!

D.S.—O the unsearchable rich-es of Christ! Precious, more precious than gold.

CHORUS.
Precious, more precious,—Wealth that can nev-er be told;

Copyright, 1882, by JOHN J. HOOD.

125. Beulah Land.

1 I'VE reached the land of corn and wine,
And all its riches freely mine;
Here shines undimmed one blissful day,
For all my night has passed away.

CHO.—O Beulah land, sweet Beulah land,
As on thy highest mount I stand,
I look away across the sea,
Where mansions are prepared for me,
And view the shining glory shore,
My heaven, my home, for evermore!

2 My Saviour comes and walks with me,
And sweet communion here have we,
He gently leads me by his hand,
For this is heaven's border-land.

3 A sweet perfume upon the breeze
Is borne from ever-vernal trees,
And flowers that never-fading grow
Where streams of life forever flow.

4 The zephyrs seem to float to me
Sweet sounds of heaven's melody,
As angels with the white-robed throng
Join in the sweet redemption song.

126. The Cleansing Blood.

CHAS. J. BUTLER.   Dr. H. L. GILMOUR.

1. Round Christ, the great incar-nate God, My arms of faith and love entwine;
2. Long sin's disease oppressed my soul,—The world could give no healing balm,—
3. A joy to unwashed souls unknown His cleansing blood has brought to me,
4. The vir-tue of my Saviour's blood To guil-ty souls I will proclaim,

His blood, for ev'-ry sinner spilt, Now cleanseth this poor heart of mine.
But now the wondrous cure I've found, In Christ the sac-ri-fi-cial lamb.
And on my peaceful spir-it shines The light that beams from Cal-va-ry.
With joyful haste I'll spread abroad Je-sus the great Phy-si-cian's fame.

D.S.—I now have found the healing balm, In Calv'ry's precious, bleeding Lamb.

CHORUS.

Oh, yes, his blood, for sinners spilt, Now cleanseth me from sin and guilt;

Copyright, 1881, by JOHN J. HOOD.

127. O for a heart to praise my God.
Tune, AVON. C. M.

1 O for a heart to praise my God,
 A heart from sin set free!
A heart that always feels thy blood,
 So freely spilt for me!

2 A heart resigned, submissive, meek,
 My great Redeemer's throne;
Where only Christ is heard to speak,
 Where Jesus reigns alone.

3 O for a lowly, contrite heart,
 Believing, true, and clean,

Which neither life nor death can part
 From him that dwells within?

4 A heart in every thought renewed,
 And full of love divine;
Perfect, and right, and pure, and good,
 A copy, Lord, of thine.

5 Thy nature, gracious Lord, impart;
 Come quickly from above;
Write thy new name upon my heart,
 Thy new, best name of love.

—CHARLES WESLEY

128. Precious Stream.

H. L. G.   H. L. Gilmour.

1. A stream from Calv'ry's summit rolls, Where all the wea-ry, wand'ring souls,
2. That stream of liv-ing wa-ter flows Where oft' the wea-ry pil-grim goes,
3. Flow on, thou stream; oh, ceaseless flow, "Till ev'-ry child of sin and woe
4. Oh! thoughtless soul, why lon-ger wait? Why tri-fle on the brink of fate?

And who-so-ev-er thirsts to-day, May drink, and find Christ precious.
To drink, and quench his rag-ing thirst, And find his Sa-viour precious.
Hath plunged beneath thy cleansing tide, And found the Sa-viour precious.
That stream still flows for you and me, Oh, come and find Christ precious.

CHORUS.

Oh! precious Je-sus, Rock for me, Stream in a des-ert, boundless, free;
I love to drink, and sat-is-fy My thirsting soul with Je-sus.

Copyright, 1881, by John J. Hood.

129. To thy cross, dear Christ, I'm clinging.   Key Eb.

1 To thy cross, dear Christ, I'm clinging,
   All my refuge and my plea;
   Matchless is thy loving kindness,
   Else it had not stooped to me.

Cho—Oh, 'tis glory! oh, 'tis glory!
   Oh, 'tis glory in my soul,
   For I've touched the hem of his garment,
   And his power doth make me whole.

2 Long my heart hath heard thee calling,
   But I thrust aside thy grace,
   Yet, O boundless condescension,
   Love is shining from thy face.

3 Love eternal, light eternal,
   Close me safely, sweetly in;
   Saviour, let thy balm of healing,
   Ever keep me free from sin.

—Mrs. E. Codner.

131. Hide Thou Me.

FANNY J. CROSBY.   "Thou art my hiding place."—Ps. xxxii. 7.   ROBERT LOWRY. By per.

1. In thy cleft, O Rock of a-ges, Hide thou me; When the fitful tempest rages, Hide thou me; Where no mortal arm can sever From my heart thy love forever, Hide me, O thou Rock of a-ges, Safe in thee.
2. From the snare of sinful pleasure, Hide thou me; Thou, my soul's eternal treasure, Hide thou me; When the world its power is wielding, And my heart is almost yielding, Hide me, O thou Rock of a-ges, Safe in thee.
3. In the lonely night of sorrow, Hide thou me; Till in glory dawns the morrow, Hide thou me; In the sight of Jordan's billow, Let thy bosom be my pillow; Hide me, O thou Rock of a-ges, Safe in thee.

132. Jesus shall reign.

1 Jesus shall reign where'er the sun
Does his successive journeys run;
His kingdom spread from shore to shore,
Till moons shall wax and wane no more.

2 From north to south the princes meet,
To pay their homage at his feet;
While western empires own their Lord,
And savage tribes attend his word.

3 To him shall endless prayer be made,
And endless praises crown his head;
His name like sweet perfume shall rise
With every morning sacrifice.

4 People and realms of every tongue
Dwell on his love with sweetest song,
And infant voices shall proclaim
Their early blessings on his name.

133. O Rest, Sweet Rest.

Martha J. Lankton.   Wm. J. Kirkpatrick.

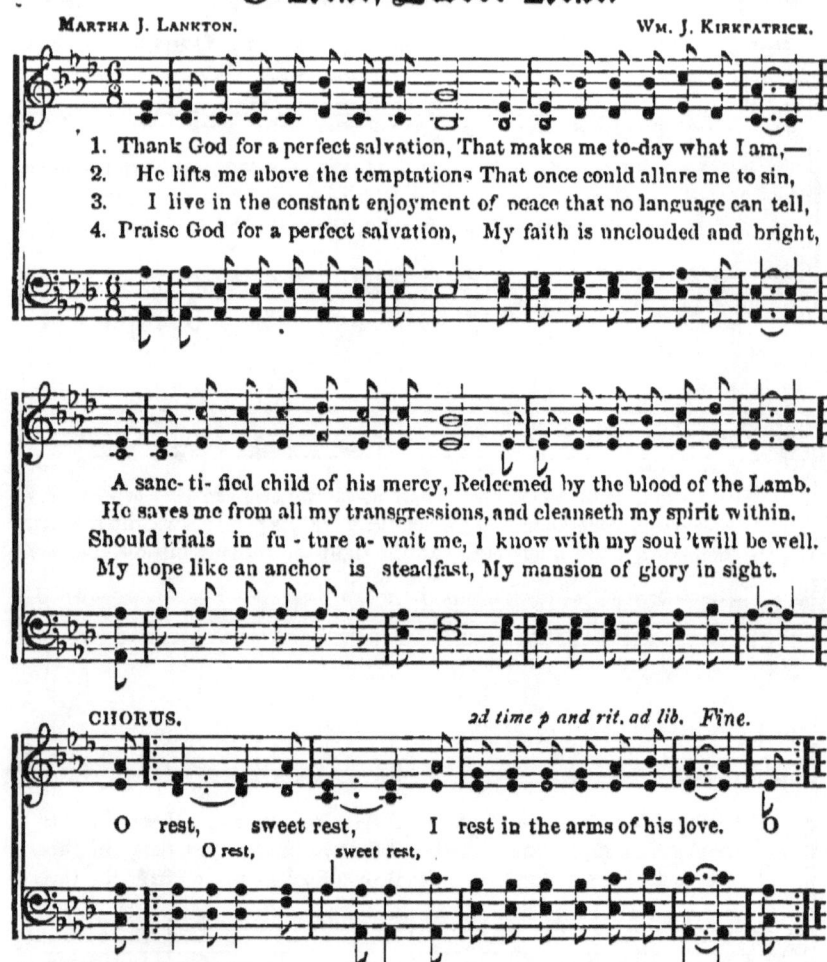

1. Thank God for a perfect salvation, That makes me to-day what I am,—
2. He lifts me above the temptations That once could allure me to sin,
3. I live in the constant enjoyment of peace that no language can tell,
4. Praise God for a perfect salvation, My faith is unclouded and bright,

A sanc-ti-fied child of his mercy, Redeemed by the blood of the Lamb.
He saves me from all my transgressions, and cleanseth my spirit within.
Should trials in fu-ture a-wait me, I know with my soul 'twill be well.
My hope like an anchor is steadfast, My mansion of glory in sight.

CHORUS.   *2d time p and rit. ad lib.*   Fine.

O rest, sweet rest, I rest in the arms of his love.
O rest, sweet rest,

Copyright, 1885, by Wm. J. Kirkpatrick.

134. The Cross! the Cross!

1 THE cross! the cross! the blood-stained cross
   The hallowed cross I see,
Reminding me of precious blood
   That once was shed for me.

Cho.—Oh, the blood! the precious blood!
   That Jesus shed for me
Upon the cross in crimson flood,
   Just now by faith I see.

2 A thousand thousand fountains spring
   Up from the throne of God;
But none to me such blessings bring,
   As Jesus' precious blood.

3 That precious blood my ransom paid
   While I in bondage stood;
On Jesus all my sins were laid;
   He saved me with his blood.

4 By faith that blood now sweeps away
   My sins, as like a flood;
Nor lets one guilty blemish stay;
   All praise to Jesus blood.

5 This wondrous theme will best employ
   My harp before my God, [joy,—
And make all heaven resound with
   My Jesus crucified.
              —Rev. Wm. McDonald.

135. His Yoke is Easy.

Ps. xxiii. R. E. Hudson.

1. The Lord is my Shepherd, I shall not want, He maketh me down to lie In pastures green, He leadeth me The qui-et wa-ters by.
2. My soul crieth out: "restore me again, And give me the strength to take The narrow path of righteousness, E'en for his own name's sake."
3. Yea, tho' I should walk in the valley of death, Yet why should I fear from ill? For thou art with me, and thy rod And staff me comfort still.

CHORUS.

His yoke is eas-y, His burden is light, I've found it so, I've found it so; He lead-eth me, by day and by night, Where living waters flow.

Copyright, 1885, by R. E. Hudson.

136. Oh, now I see the cleansing wave!

Key Eb.

1 Oh, now I see the cleansing wave!
  The fountain deep and wide;
  Jesus, my Lord, mighty to save,
  Points to his wounded side.

Cho—The cleansing stream I see, I see!
  I plunge, and oh, it cleanseth me!
  Oh, praise the Lord! it cleanseth me!
  It cleanseth me—yes, cleanseth me.

2 I rise to walk in heaven's own light,
  Above the world of sin,   [white,
  With heart made pure, and garments
  And Christ enthroned within.

3 Amazing grace! 'tis heaven below
  To feel the blood applied;
  And Jesus, only Jesus, know,
  My Jesus crucified.

137 We'll Sound the Loud Timbrel.

[Repeat four times for each verse.]

REFRAIN.

We'll sound the loud timbrel o'er Egypt's dark sea; Jehovah has triumphed, his people are free.

1. My soul's full of glory,
   Inspiring my tongue,
   Could I meet with angels
   I'd sing them a song;
   I'd sing of my Jesus,
   And tell of his charms
   And beg them to bear me
   To his loving arms.

2. I find him in singing,
   I find him in prayer;
   In sweet meditation
   He always is there.
   My constant companion,
   Oh, may we ne'er part!
   All glory to Jesus,
   He dwells in my heart.

3. Oh, who is like Jesus!
   He's Salem's bright King!
   He smiles, and he loves me,
   And helps me to sing:
   I'll praise him, I'll praise him,
   Whatever his will,
   While rivers of pleasure
   My spirit doth fill.

138 Holiness—An Experience.

Arranged for this work.

D.S.—We will lay our burdens down, And a starry crown shall wear
And at Jesus' feet sit down, Over there!

CHORUS.   *D S.*

Over there, over there, Over there, over there, There's a land of pure delight Over there!

1. I am walking in the light,
   And the path is shining bright,
   Where there is no more of night
   I now dwell;
   This vain world I bid adieu,
   And its glories fade from view;
   I have found earth all untrue,
   It is well.

2. I have garments wrought of gold,
   And their value is untold,
   They have neither moth nor mold,
   Bless the Lord!
   I have jewels rich and rare,
   And a mansion bright and fair,
   For his will is written there
   In his word.

3. I have angels' food to eat,
   And no honey is so sweet;
   It is most delicious meat
   For the soul.
   In his promise I abide,
   And my soul is satisfied,
   While I feel the crimson tide
   O'er me roll.

4. I have glory for a prize,
   And a crown beyond the skies,
   When from earth I shall arise,
   Pure and white.
   I shall then with Jesus reign,
   And eternal honor gain,
   And be pure from every stain
   In his sight.

139. Full Salvation.

F. H. Steele. E. E. Nickerson.

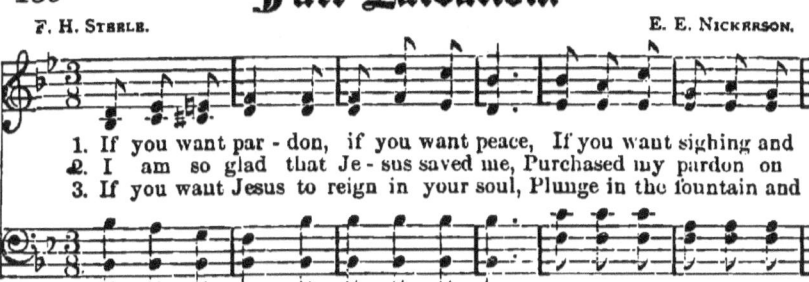

1. If you want par-don, if you want peace, If you want sighing and
2. I am so glad that Je-sus saved me, Purchased my pardon on
3. If you want Jesus to reign in your soul, Plunge in the fountain and

Cho.—Liv-ing be-neath the shade of the cross, Counting the jew-els of

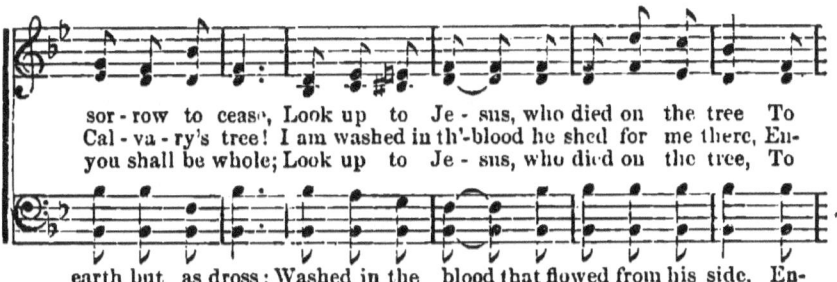

sor-row to cease, Look up to Je-sus, who died on the tree To
Cal-va-ry's tree! I am washed in th'-blood he shed for me there, En-
you shall be whole; Look up to Je-sus, who died on the tree, To

earth but as dross; Washed in the blood that flowed from his side, En-

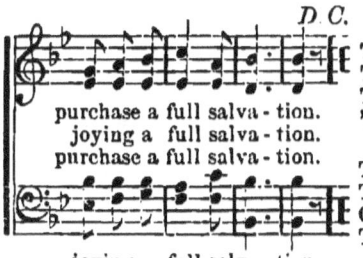

D.C.

purchase a full salva-tion.
joying a full salva-tion.
purchase a full salva-tion.

joying a full salva-tion.

4
There's peace in believing, sweet peace to the soul,
To know that he maketh me perfectly whole;
There's joy everlasting to feel his blood flow,
'Tis life my Redeemer to know.

5
There's peace in believing, sweet peace to the soul,
To know that he maketh me perfectly whole;
Oh, come to the fountain, oh, come at his call,
There's healing and cleansing for all.

From "Highway Songs," by per.

140. Lord, I hear of showers of blessing. Key G.

1 Lord, I hear of showers of blessing
  Thou art scattering full and free—
  Showers the thirsty land refreshing;
  Let some drops now fall on me.

Ref.—Even me, even me,
  Let some drops now fall on me.

2 Pass me not, O God, my Father!
  Sinful though my heart may be;
  Thou mightst leave me, but the rather,
  Let thy mercy light on me.

3 Pass me not, O gracious Saviour!
  Let me live and cling to thee;
  I am longing for thy favor;
  Whilst thou 'rt calling, oh, call me.

4 Pass me not, O mighty Spirit!
  Thou canst make the blind to see;
  Witnesser of Jesus' merit,
  Speak the word of power to me.

Ref.—Even me, even me,
  Let some drops now fall on me.

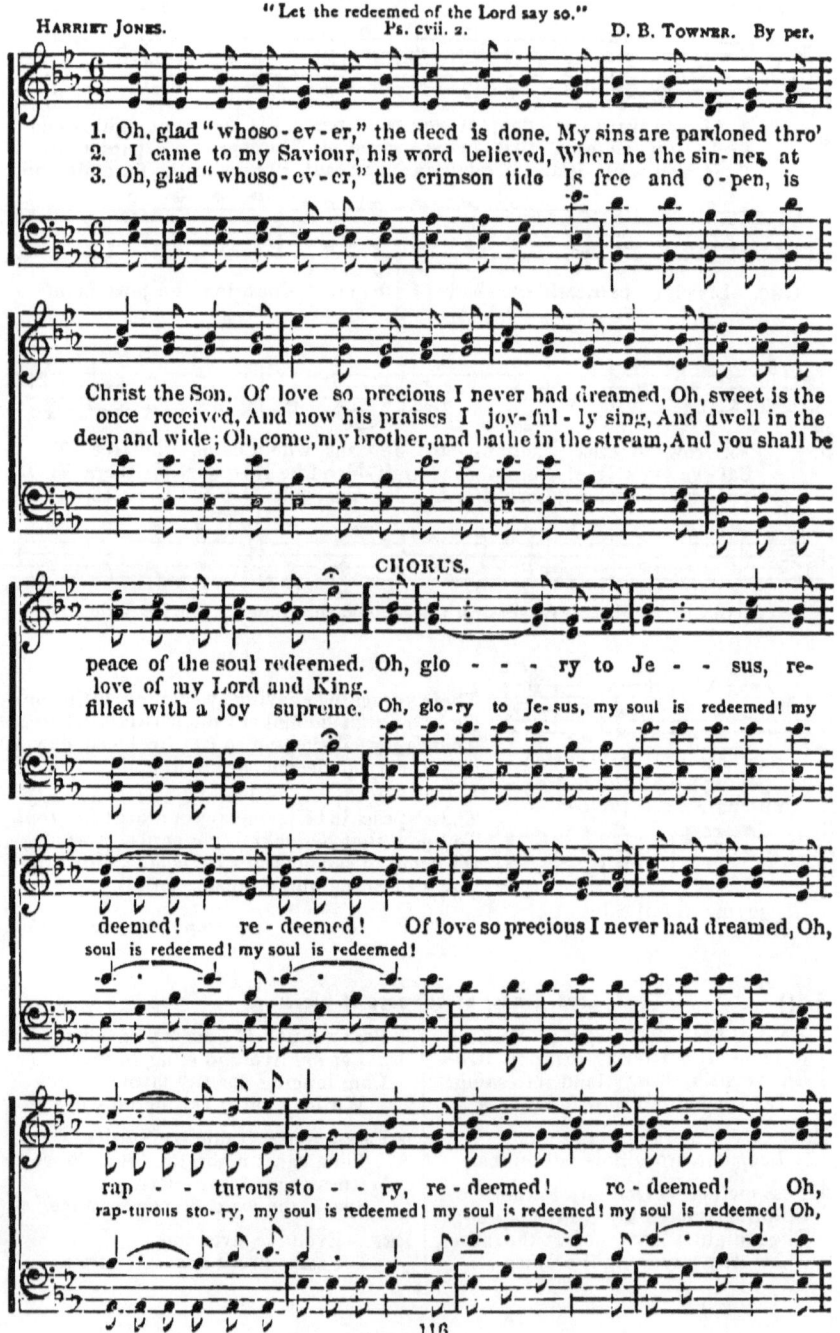

144. Surrendered.

H. L. G. — Dr. H. L. Gilmour.

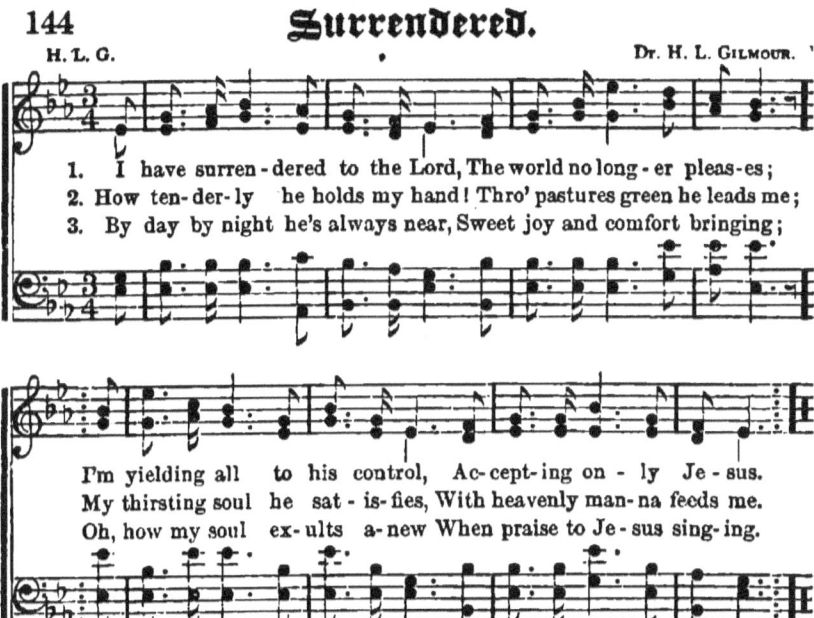

1. I have surren-dered to the Lord, The world no long-er pleas-es;
2. How ten-der-ly he holds my hand! Thro' pastures green he leads me;
3. By day by night he's always near, Sweet joy and comfort bringing;

I'm yielding all to his control, Ac-cept-ing on - ly Je - sus.
My thirsting soul he sat - is- fies, With heavenly man-na feeds me.
Oh, how my soul ex-ults a-new When praise to Je-sus sing-ing.

4 No noonday drought affects my soul,
In Jesus I'm confiding;
Oh, constant, sweet companionship,
With Christ in me abiding.

5 Oh, victory that's always sure!
Oh, blest emancipation!
Oh, vanquished tempter of my soul!
Oh, free and full salvation!

145. Dear Jesus, I long to be perfectly whole.

Key Eb.

1 Dear Jesus, I long to be perfectly whole;
I want thee forever to live in my soul:
Break down every idol, cast out every foe;
Now wash me, and I shall be whiter than snow.

CHO.—Whiter than snow, yes, whiter than snow:
Now wash me, and I shall be whiter than snow;

2 Dear Jesus, let nothing unholy remain;
Apply thine own blood, and remove every stain;
To have this blest cleansing, I all things forego;
Now wash me, and I shall be whiter than snow.

3 Dear Jesus, come down from thy throne in the skies,
And help me to make a complete sacrifice;
I give up myself, and whatever I know:
Now wash me, and I shall be whiter than snow.

4 Dear Jesus, thou seest I patiently wait;
Come now and within me a clean heart create;
To those who have sought thee thou never saidst no,
Now wash me, and I shall be whiter than snow.

5 Dear Jesus, for this I most humbly entreat;
I wait, blessed Lord, at thy crucified feet;
By faith, for my cleansing I see thy blood flow:
Now wash me, and I shall be whiter than snow.

6 The blessing by faith I receive from above:
O glory! my soul is made perfect in love:
My prayer has prevailed, and this moment I know
The blood is applied; I am whiter than snow. —Jas. Nicholson.

146. Thou Wast Smitten.

F. G. Burroughs.
With feeling.
Isaiah liii. 4.
H. L. Gilmour.

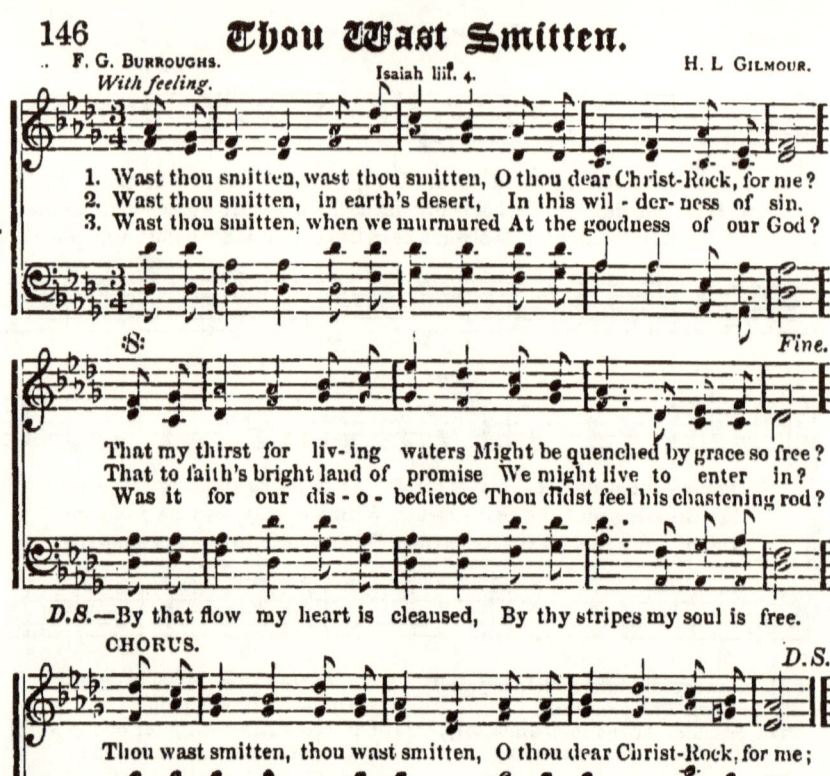

1. Wast thou smitten, wast thou smitten, O thou dear Christ-Rock, for me?
2. Wast thou smitten, in earth's desert, In this wil-der-ness of sin.
3. Wast thou smitten, when we murmured At the goodness of our God?

That my thirst for liv-ing waters Might be quenched by grace so free?
That to faith's bright land of promise We might live to enter in?
Was it for our dis-o-bedience Thou didst feel his chastening rod?

D.S.—By that flow my heart is cleansed, By thy stripes my soul is free.

CHORUS.

Thou wast smitten, thou wast smitten, O thou dear Christ-Rock, for me;

4 Wast thou smitten, just to save us
From the death our sin decreed?
Was thy body pierced and riven
Till thy very soul did bleed?

5 Wast thou smitten, my Beloved,
That I might behold thy love,
And henceforth set my affections
On the things that are above?

Copyright, 1889, by H. L. Gilmour.

147. What poor despised company.

Key F.

1 What poor despised company
Of travelers are these,
Who walk in yonder narrow way,
Along that rugged maze?
Cho.—I had rather be the least of them,
Who are the Lord's alone,
‖: Than wear a royal diadem,
‖: And sit upon a throne. :‖

2 Ah! these are of a royal line,
All children of a King!
Heirs of immortal crowns divine,
And lo! for joy they sing.

3 Why do they then appear so mean?
And why so much despised?
Because of their rich robes unseen
The world is not apprised.

4 But some of them seem poor, distressed,
And lacking daily bread: [sessed,
Ah! they're of boundless wealth pos-
With heavenly manna fed,

5 Why do they shun the pleasing path
That worldlings love so well?
Because it is the way to death:
The open road to hell.

6 But why keep they the narrow road,
That rugged, thorny maze?
Why, that's the way their Leader trod;
They love and keep his ways.

7 What, is there then no other road
To Salem's happy ground?
Christ is the only way to God:
None other can be found.

148. I'll be There.

ISAAC WATTS.   Adapted by WM. J. KIRKPATRICK.

1. There is a land of pure delight, Where saints immor-tal reign;
   In-fi-nite day ex-cludes the night, And pleasures ban-ish pain.
2. There ev-er-last-ing spring abides, And nev-er-with'ring flowers;
   Death, like a narrow sea, divides This heavenly land from ours.

REFRAIN.
I'll be there, I'll be there, When the first trumpet sounds I'll be there,
I'll be there,
I'll be there, I'll be there, When the first trumpet sounds I'll be there.

3 Sweet fields beyond the swelling flood
  Stand dressed in living green;
  So to the Jews old Canaan stood,
  While Jordan rolled between.

4 Could we but climb where Moses stood,
  And view the landscape o'er,
  Not Jordan's stream, nor death's cold flood
  Should fright us from the shore.

Copyright, 1887, by WM. J. KIRKPATRICK.

---

149.   Down at the cross, where my Saviour died.   Key Ab.

1 Down at the cross, where my Saviour died,
  Down where for cleansing from sin I cried;
  There to my heart was the blood applied;
    Glory to his name.

CHO.—Glory to his name,
    Glory to his name,
  There to my heart was the blood applied;
    Glory to his name.

2 I am so wondrously saved from sin,
  Jesus so sweetly abides within;

  There at the cross where he took me in;
    Glory to his name.

3 Oh, precious fountain, that saves from sin,
  I am so glad I have entered in;
  There Jesus saves me and keeps me clean,
    Glory to his name.

4 Come to this fountain, so rich and sweet;
  Cast thy poor soul at the Saviour's feet;
  Plunge in to-day, and be made complete;
    Glory to his name.

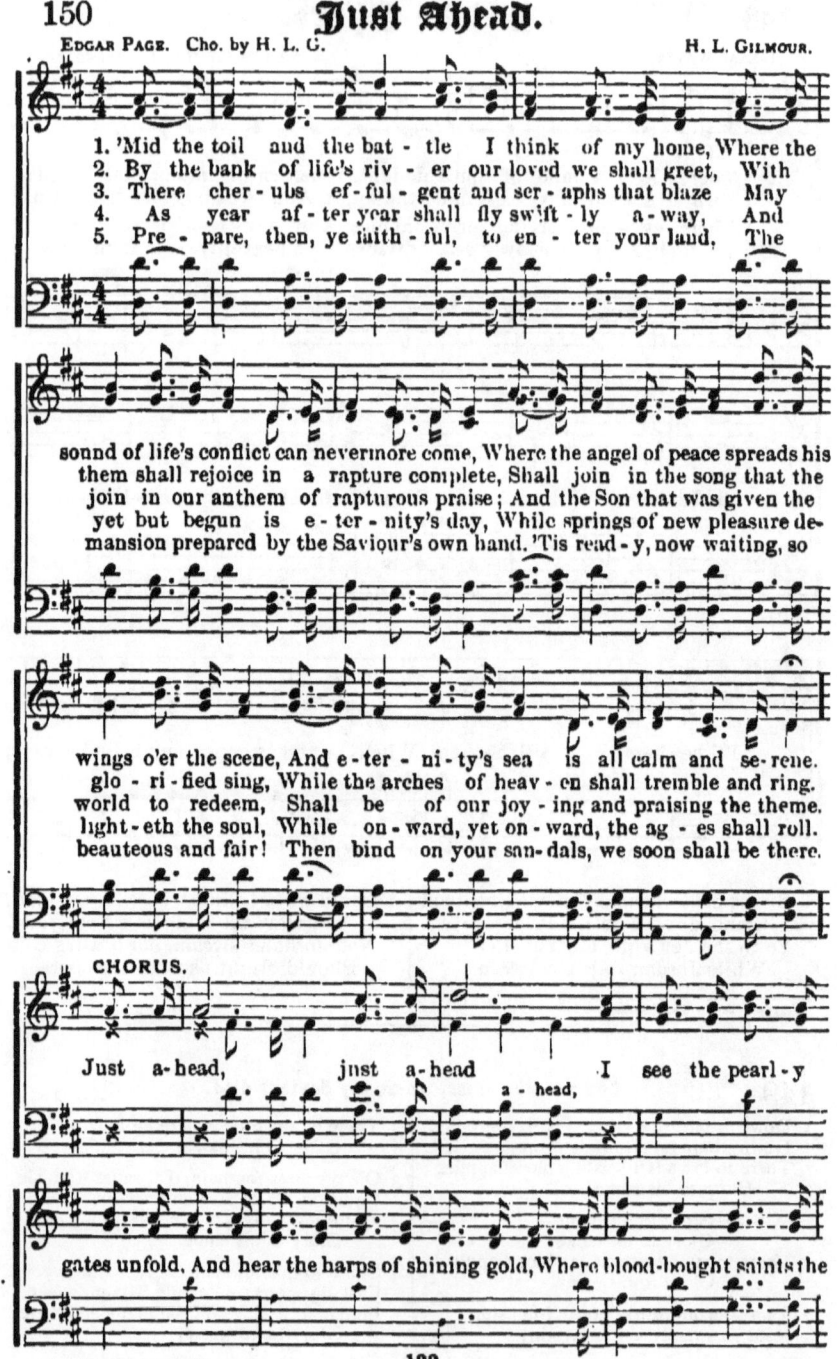

Just Ahead.—CONCLUDED.

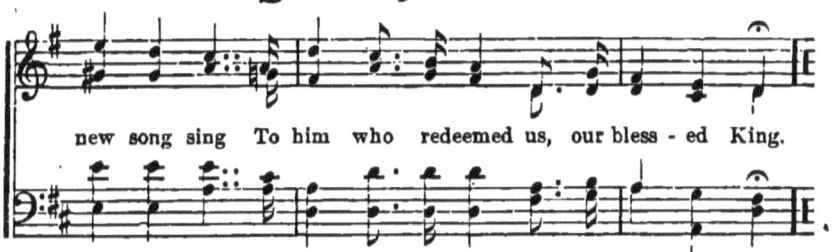

new song sing To him who redeemed us, our bless-ed King.

On the Cross.

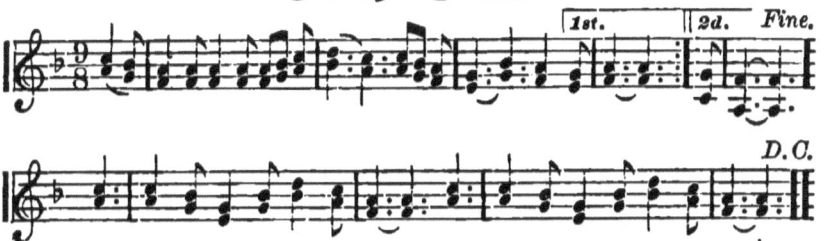

151 Behold! behold the Lamb.

1 Behold! behold the Lamb of God,
  On the cross, on the cross;
For you he shed his precious blood,
  On the cross, on the cross.
Now hear his agonizing cry,
"Eloi lama sabacthani:"
Draw near and see your Saviour die,
  On the cross, on the cross.

2 Come, sinners, see him lifted up,
  On the cross, on the cross;
He drinks for you the bitter cup,
  On the cross, on the cross.
To heaven he turns his languid eyes,
"'Tis finished," now the conqueror cries,
Then bows his sacred head and dies,
  On the cross, on the cross.

3 'Tis done! the mighty deed is done,
  On the cross, on the cross;
The battle fought, the victory won,
  On the cross, on the cross.
The rocks do rend, the mountains quake,
While Jesus doth atonement make,
While Jesus suffers for your sake,
  On the cross, on the cross.

4 Where'er I go I'll tell the story,
  Of the cross, of the cross;
In nothing else my soul shall glory,
  Save the cross, save the cross.
Yes, this my constant theme shall be,
Through time, and in eternity,
That Jesus suffered death for me,
  On the cross, on the cross.

152 By faith I view my Saviour.

1 By faith I view my Saviour dying,
  On thee tree, on the tree;
To every nation he is crying,
  Look to me, look to me.
He bids the guilty now draw near,
Repent, believe, dismiss their fear;
Hark, hark, what precious words I hear,
  Mercy's free, mercy's free.

2 Did Christ, when I was sin pursuing,
  Pity me, pity me?
And did he snatch my soul from ruin?
  Can it be, can it be?
Oh, yes! he did salvation bring;
He is my Prophet, Priest, and King;
And now my happy soul can sing,
  Mercy's free, mercy's free.

3 Jesus my weary soul refreshes;
  Mercy's free, mercy's free,
And every moment Christ is precious
  Unto me, unto me.
None can describe the bliss I prove,
While through this wilderness I rove,
All may enjoy the Saviour's love,
  Mercy's free, mercy's free.

4 Long as I live, I'll still be crying,
  Mercy's free, mercy's free;
And this shall be my theme when dying,
  Mercy's free, mercy's free.
And when the vale of death I've passed,
When lodged above the stormy blast,
I'll sing, while endless ages last,
  Mercy's free, mercy's free.

Alway.—CONCLUDED.

My soul he will nev-er, No, nev-er, no, nev-er for-sake.

---

154 R. K. C. **The Blood's Applied.** R. Kelso Carter.
Fine.

1. { The blood's applied! my soul is free, I'm saved, without, with-in;
   { The blood of Je-sus cleanseth me From ev-'ry trace of sin. }

D. S.—blood's applied, I'm sanc-ti-fied, It makes me pure with-in.

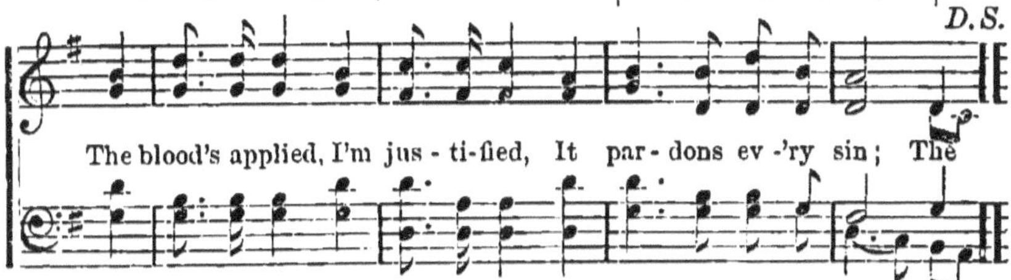

D. S.

The blood's applied, I'm jus-ti-fied, It par-dons ev-'ry sin; The

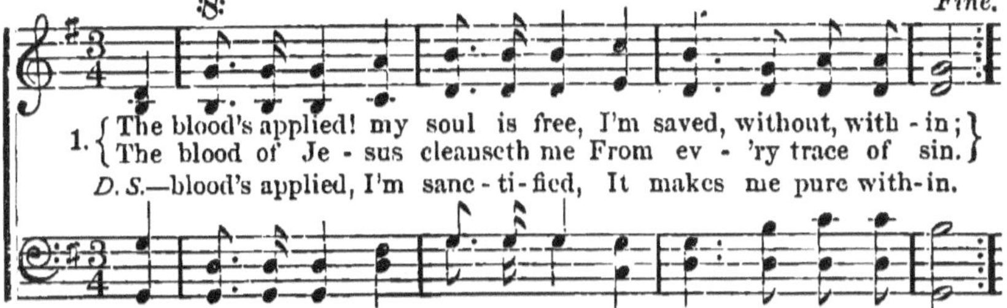

2 I've bid farewell to every fear,
   By faith I claim the prize;
   Now I can read my title clear
   To mansions in the skies.

3 Temptations come and trials too,
   While hellish darts are hurled;
   But Jesus saves me through and
   In spite of all the world. [through,

4 Though cares and storms and sorrows
   About me thick and fast, [fall
   My Jesus,—he is Lord of all,—
   Will bring me home at last.

5 Then will my happy, happy soul
   Tell of his love and rest,
   While shouts of victory shall roll
   From every conquering breast.

Copyright, 1886, by John J. Hood.

---

155 I. Watts. **Am I a Soldier of the Cross?** *Tune above.*

1 Am I a soldier of the cross,
   A follower of the Lamb,
   And shall I fear to own his cause,
   Or blush to speak his name?

2 Must I be carried to the skies
   On flowery beds of ease,
   While others fought to win the prize,
   And sailed through bloody seas?

3 Are there no foes for me to face?
   Must I not stem the flood?
   Is this vile world a friend to grace,
   To help me on to God?

4 Sure I must fight, if I would reign;
   Increase my courage, Lord;
   I'll bear the toil, endure the pain,
   Supported by thy word.

5 Thy saints in all this glorious war
   Shall conquer, though they die:
   They see the triumph from afar,
   By faith they bring it nigh.

6 When that illustrious day shall rise,
   And all thy armies shine
   In robes of victory through the skies,
   The glory shall be thine.

156. The Stranger at the Door.

Rev. iii. 20.

T. C. O'Kane.

1. Behold a stranger at the door, He gently knocks—has knocked before,
Has waited long, is waiting still; You treat no other friend so ill.

2. O lovely attitude,—he stands With melting heart and open hands;
O matchless kindness, and he shows This matchless kindness to his foes.

3. But will he prove a friend indeed? He will,—the very friend you need;
The friend of sinners? Yes, 'tis he, With garments dyed on Calvary.

CHORUS.

Oh, let the dear Saviour come in, He'll cleanse the heart from sin; Oh, keep him no more out at the door, But let the dear Saviour come in.

4 Rise, touched with gratitude divine,
Turn out his enemy and thine;
That soul-destroying monster, Sin,
And let the heavenly Stranger in.

5 Admit him, ere his anger burn,—
His feet, departed, ne'er return;
Admit him, or the hour's at hand
You'll at HIS door rejected stand.

By permission.

INVITATION HYMNS.

159 Come, Believer.

1 COME, believer, hung'ring, thirsting,
　Come, a living sacrifice,
　God will sanctify you wholly,
　　Cleanse and fit you for the skies.

Cho.—Come to the cross for full salvation,
　Now the Comforter receive,
　Perfect peace, and full salvation
　　God the Holy Ghost will give.

2 Now, believer, come and welcome,
　God's free bounty glorify,
　Come in faith and consecration,
　　All your fleshly hopes deny.

3 Lo! the Holy Ghost descending!
　Now behold the cleansing blood,
　Venture on him, venture freely,
　　Plunge beneath the crimson flood.

4 Christ the Comforter has promised
　To the pardoned child of God,
　Oh, believer, come and seek him,
　　Let your soul be his abode.

5 He will 'stablish, fix and keep you,
　Rooted, grounded in his love,
　Calm your wav'ring heart and seal it,
　　Seal it for his courts above.

6 Into all his truth he'll lead you,
　All things teach you as you go,
　In the dying hour be with you,
　　Death's dark river guide you through.

160 Come, thou Fount.

1 COME, thou Fount of every blessing,
　Tune my heart to sing thy grace,
　Streams of mercy, never ceasing,
　　Call for songs of loudest praise.

2 Teach me some melodious sonnet,
　Sung by flaming tongues above;
　Praise the mount—I'm fixed upon it—
　　Mount of thy redeeming love!

3 Here I'll raise my Ebenezer;
　Hither by thy help I'm come;
　And I hope, by thy good pleasure,
　　Safely to arrive at home.

4 Jesus sought me when a stranger,
　Wandering from the fold of God;
　He, to rescue me from danger,
　　Interposed his precious blood.

161 Oh, turn ye.

1 OH, turn ye, oh, turn ye, for why will ye die,
When God in great mercy is coming so nigh?
Since Jesus invites you, the Spirit says, come!
And angels are waiting to welcome you home.

2 How vain the delusion, that while you delay,
Your hearts may grow better by staying away;
Come wretched, come starving, come just as
　you be,
While streams of salvation are flowing so free.

3 And now Christ is ready your souls to receive,
Oh, how can you question, if you will believe?
If sin is your burden, why will you not come?
'Tis you he bids welcome; he bids you come
　home.

4 In riches, in pleasures, what can you obtain
To soothe your affliction, or banish your pain,
To bear up your spirit when summoned to die,
Or waft you to mansions of glory on high?

5 Why will you be starving and feeding on air?
There's mercy in Jesus, enough and to spare;
If still you are doubting make trial and see,
And prove that his mercy is boundless and free.

6 Come, give us your hand, and the Saviour
　your heart,
And, trusting in heaven, we never shall part;
Oh, how can we leave you? why will you not
　come?
We'll journey together, and soon be at home.

162 Only Trust Him.

1 COME, every soul by sin oppressed,
　There's mercy with the Lord,
　And he will surely give you rest,
　　By trusting in his word.

Cho.—Only trust him, only trust him,
　Only trust him now;
　He will save you, he will save you,
　　He will save you now.

2 For Jesus shed his precious blood,
　Rich blessings to bestow;
　Plunge now into the crimson flood
　　That washes white as snow.

3 Yes, Jesus is the Truth, the Way,
　That leads you into rest;
　Believe in him without delay,
　　And you are fully blest.

4 Come, then, and join this holy band,
　And on to glory go,
　To dwell in that celestial land
　　Where joys immortal flow.

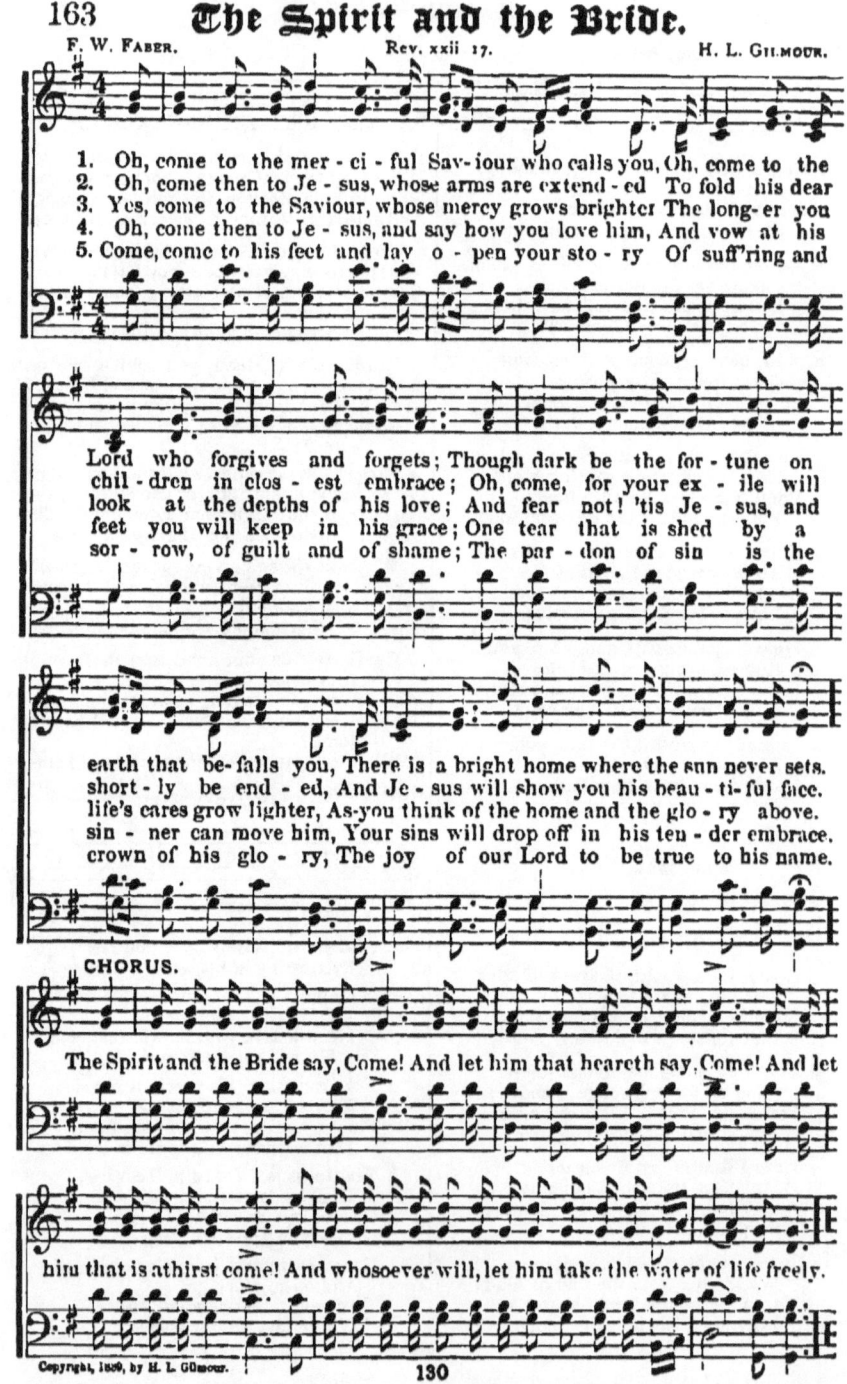

164. Salvation Full and Free.

R. K. C.   R. Kelso Carter.

1. In ev'-ry tribe and ev'-ry na-tion, All can the prom-ise trace;
   Saved by his grace, we're saved forever, Bought by his precious blood;
2. Christ leads us on, his Spir-it guiding Where the still wa-ters flow;
   From cloud and mist the sky grows lighter, Straighter the narrow way;
3. Look o'er the night of sin and sorrow, Je-sus has come to save:
   All free from sin and pain, he told us, We shall a-bide in peace;

Now is the time of God's sal-vation, This is the day of grace.
Naught can molest, and none can sev-er Us from the Son of God.
Un-der his wings in peace a-biding, Shield-ed from ev-'ry blow.
Oh, more and more the sun shines brighter Un-to the per-fect day.
Lift up your heads! a glad to-morrow Ris-es a-bove the grave.
Ev-er the arms of love en-fold us, Ev-er all trou-ble cease.

CHORUS.

Broth-ers, see the Lord of glo-ry Dy-ing on the tree! Oh, shout aloud the wondrous sto-ry Of sal-va-tion so full and free.

Copyright, 1889, by R. Kelso Carter.

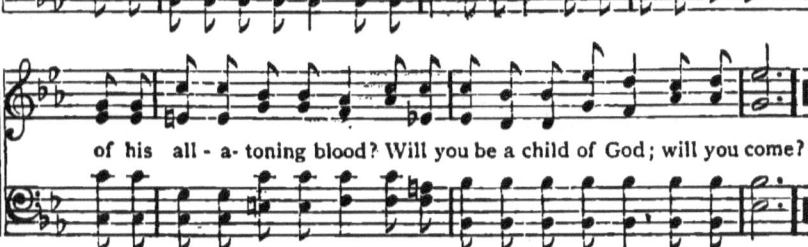

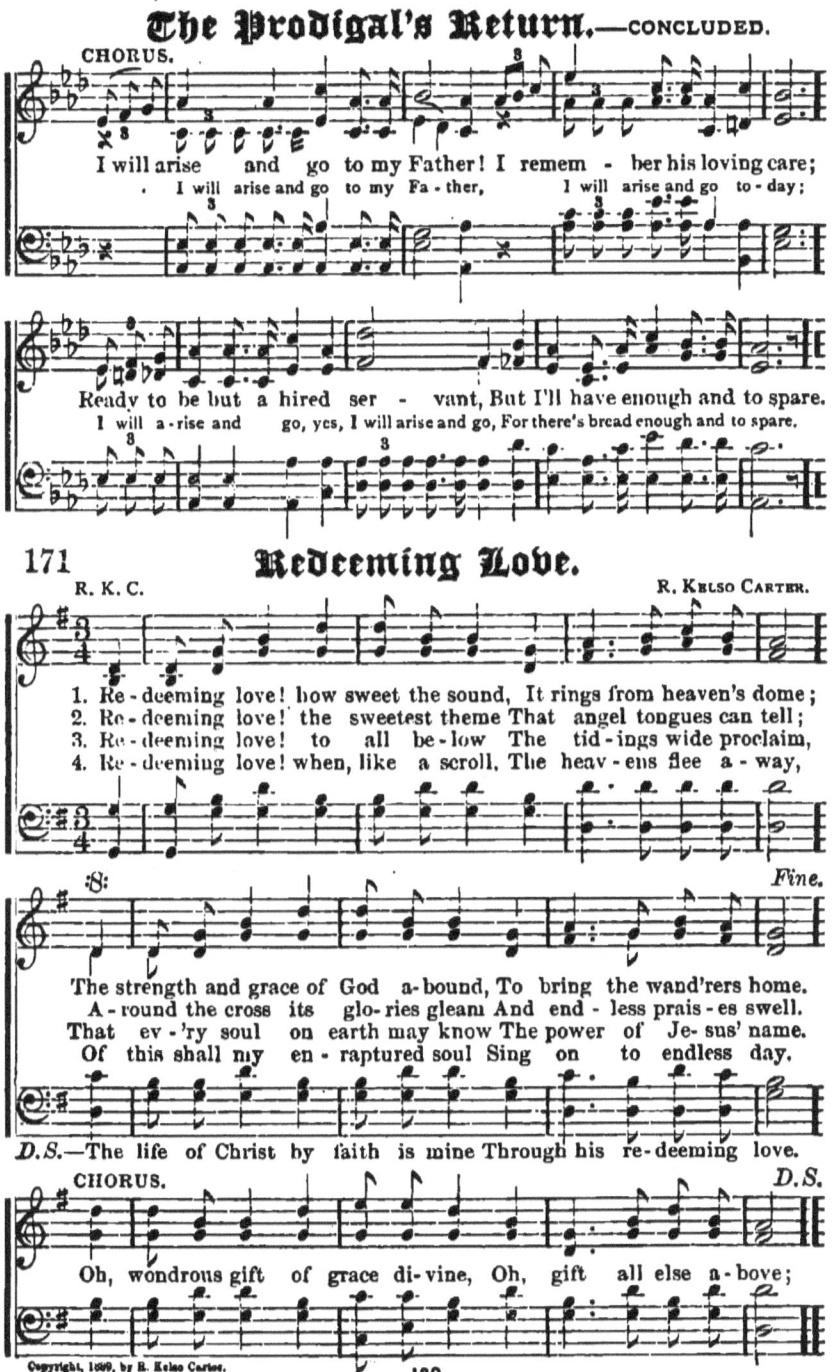

176 "I'm a Lost Man."

A GENTLEMAN, nearly crazy with trouble and the conviction of sin, walked his parlor floor almost continually day and night for a week, crying incessantly, "I'm lost! I'm lost!" So long had the walk been kept up that he had worn a distinct path in the carpet; and always the same distressing cry was heard. I was called to see him, and after watching the man a few moments, I startled him into interest and attention by saying earnestly, in response to the cry, "I'm lost," "I am glad to hear it." "What! do you mean to say you are glad I'm lost?" "Yes, I am glad of it." In utter amazement the man asked, "How can you be glad of such a thing?" "Because," said I, "Jesus Christ came to seek and to save that which was lost." And in a very few minutes on our knees in simple prayer light broke into the darkened soul, and in his right mind, the man arose praising God that he was found.—Dr. CHARLES CULLIS.

H L. G.   H. L. GILMOUR.

1. I'm lost! I'm lost! The ech-o seems so sad; How hopeless is my fate!
2. I'll trust, I'll trust, The Saviour now invites, In ten - der, pleading tone,
3. I'm saved! I'm saved! The Father now forgives, By faith the blood's applied;

I'm lost! I'm lost! Oh, tell me, is there no escape from that . . .
Come un - to me, And, though your sins like scarlet are, they shall
I'll praise the Lord, That Christ came not to call the righteous, but

death which nev - er dies? And must I be to judgment brought?
be as white as snow; And though they be like crimson red,
sin - ners to repentance, That whosoever believeth in him should not perish,

CHORUS.

And shall I hear that sad, de - part? No; it is written, The
They shall be like un - to wool. Yes, it is written, The
But have ever - - - last - ing life. Yes, it is written, The

Copyright, 1889, by H. L. Gilmour.

"I'm a Lost Man."—CONCLUDED.

Son of man, the Son of man Came to seek, came to save, Came to seek, he came to save, Came to seek, he came to save That which was lost.

177 O Sinner, Come.

H. L. GILMOUR.   *Dedicated to Mrs. Lizzie Smith.*   Old tune and chorus.

1. O sinner, come, there's pardon free, The blood of Christ was shed for thee,
1st. CHO.—We're waiting at the mer - cy seat, We're waiting at the mer - cy seat,
2d. CHO.—I can, I will, I do believe, I can, I will, I do believe,

There is no oth - er way or plea, O wea - ry wand'rer, come.
We're wait-ing at the mer - cy seat, Where Je - sus answers prayer.
I can, I will, I do believe That Je - sus died for me.

2 O sinner, come, the feast is spread,
And Christ supplies the living bread,
And his own word has sweetly said,
  O weary wand'rer, come.

3 The poor, the maimed, the halt, the blind,
And whosoever *will*, may find
Salvation that leaves none behind,
  O weary wand'rer, come.

4 O sinner, come, he'll give thee rest,
And sweet repose upon his breast,
A constant, true, abiding guest,
  O weary wand'rer, come.

5 O sinner, come, no longer roam,
Accept the invitation—come,
The Father waits to welcome home,
  O weary wand'rer, come.

Copyright, 1889, by H. L. Gilmour.

179. God is Calling Yet.

GERHARD TERSTEEGEN.
E. O. EXCELL. By per.

1. God calling yet! shall I not hear? Earth's pleasures shall I still hold dear?
2. God calling yet! shall I not rise? Can I his lov-ing voice de-spise,
3. God calling yet! and shall he knock, And I my heart the clos-er lock?
4. God calling yet! and shall I give No heed, but still in bondage live?
5. God calling yet! I can-not stay; My heart I yield without de-lay:

Shall life's swift passing years all fly, And still my soul in slumber lie?
And base-ly his kind care re-pay? He calls me still; can I de-lay?
He still is wait-ing to re-ceive, And shall I dare his Spir-it grieve?
I wait, but he does not for-sake: He calls me still; my heart, awake!
Vain world, farewell, from thee I part; The voice of God has reach'd my heart.

CHORUS.

Call - - ing, oh, hear him, Call - - ing, oh, hear him, God is
God is call-ing yet, God is call-ing yet,

call-ing yet, oh, hear him calling, calling, Call - - ing, oh, hear him,
God is call-ing yet,

Call - - ing, oh, hear him, God is calling yet, oh, hear him calling yet.
God is calling yet,

Copyright, 1881, by E. O. Excell.

181. Come, Ye Sinners.

JOSEPH HART. Cho. by H. L. G. Tune, BARTIMEUS. 8,7.

1. Come, ye sin-ners, poor and needy, Weak and wounded, sick and sore;
D.C.—He is a-ble, He is a-ble, He is will-ing: doubt no more;
CHO.—Come to Je-sus, come to Je-sus, Mer-cy's door wide o-pen stands;

D.C.

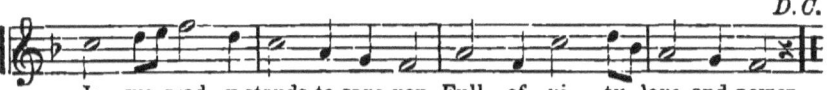

Je-sus read-y stands to save you, Full of pi-ty, love, and power.
He is a-ble, He is a-ble, He is will-ing: doubt no more.
Lov-ing-ly he waits to welcome; See his beck'ning, wounded hands.

2 Now, ye needy, come and welcome;
God's free bounty glorify;
True belief and true repentance—
Every grace that brings you nigh—
Without money,
Come to Jesus Christ and buy.

3 Let not conscience make you linger,
Nor of fitness fondly dream;
All the fitness he requireth
Is to feel your need of him.
This he gives you—
'Tis the Spirit's glimmering beam.

4 Come, ye weary, heavy laden,
Bruised and mangled by the fall,
If you tarry till you're better,
You will never come at all.
Not the righteous—
Sinners Jesus came to call.

5 Agonizing in the garden
Your Redeemer prostrate lies;
On the bloody tree behold him,
Hear him cry, before he dies,
It is finished!—
Sinners, will not this suffice?

182. And can I yet delay?

Tune No. 20.

1 AND can I yet delay
My little all to give?
To tear my soul from earth away
For Jesus to receive?

2 Nay, but I yield, I yield;
I can hold out no more:
I sink, by dying love compelled,
And own thee conqueror.

4 Come, and possess me whole,
Nor hence again remove;
Settle and fix my wavering soul
With all thy weight of love.

3 Though late I all forsake,
My friends, my all, resign;
Gracious Redeemer, take, oh, take,
And seal me ever thine.

183. Lord, I care not for riches.

Key Ab.

1 LORD, I care not for riches,
Neither silver nor gold;
I would make sure of heaven,
I would enter the fold;
In the book of thy kingdom,
With its pages so fair,
Tell me, Jesus, my Saviour,
Is my name written there?

CHO.—Is my name written there,
On the page white and fair?
In the book of thy kingdom,
Is my name written there?

Lord, my sins they are many,
Like the sands of the sea,

But thy blood, O my Saviour!
Is sufficient for me;
For thy promise is written,
In bright letters that glow,
"Though your sins be as scarlet,
I will make them like snow."

3 Oh! that beautiful city,
With its mansions of light,
With its glorified beings,
In pure garments of white;
Where no evil thing cometh,
To despoil what is fair;
Where the angels are watching,—
Is my name written there?

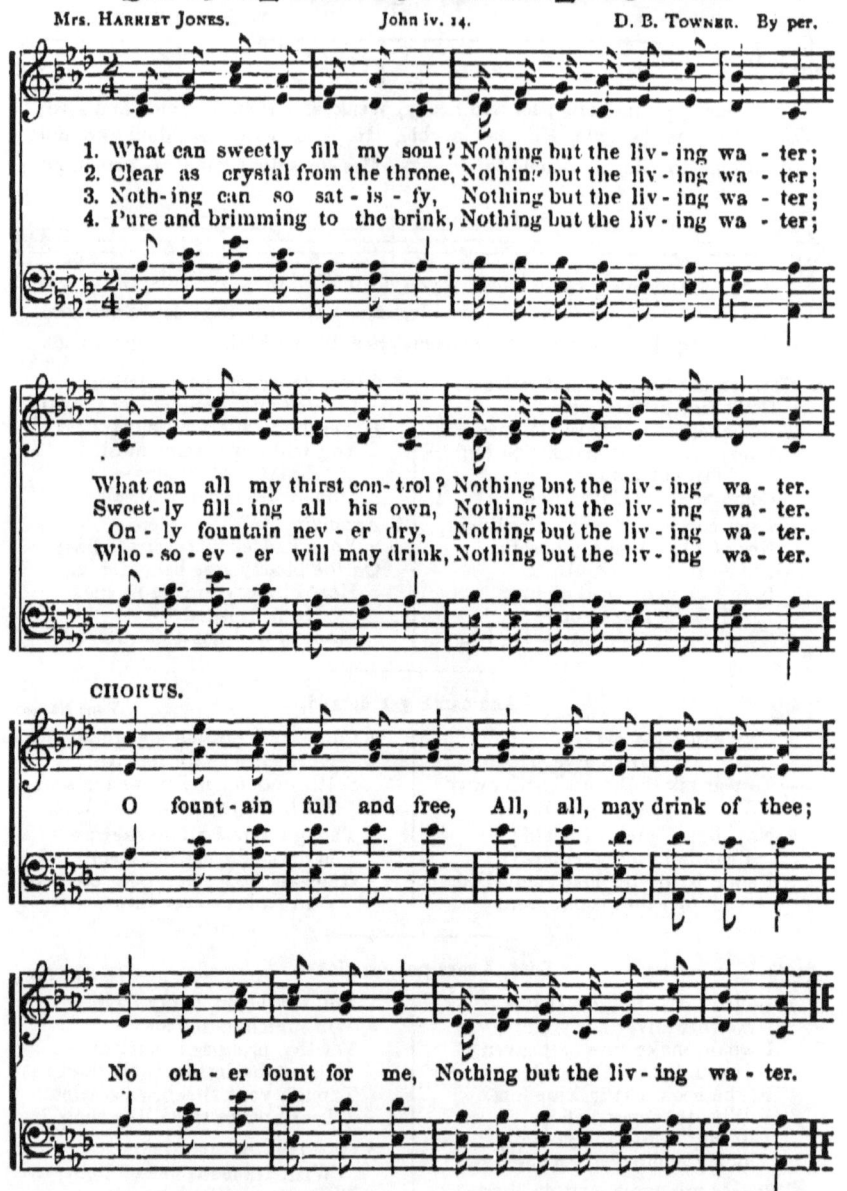

185. The Gospel Feast.

CHARLES WESLEY. "Come, for all things are ready."
Cho. by H. L. G. Luke xiv. 16. H. L. GILMOUR.

1. Come, sinners, to the gos-pel feast; It is for you, it is for me;
   Let ev'-ry soul be Je-sus' guest: It is for you, it is for me.
2. Ye need not one be left behind, It is for you, it is for me;
   For God hath bid-den all mankind, It is for you, it is for me.

D.S.—O wea-ry wand'rer, come and see, It is for you, it is for me.

CHORUS.

Sal-va-tion full, sal-vation free, The price was paid on Calva-ry;

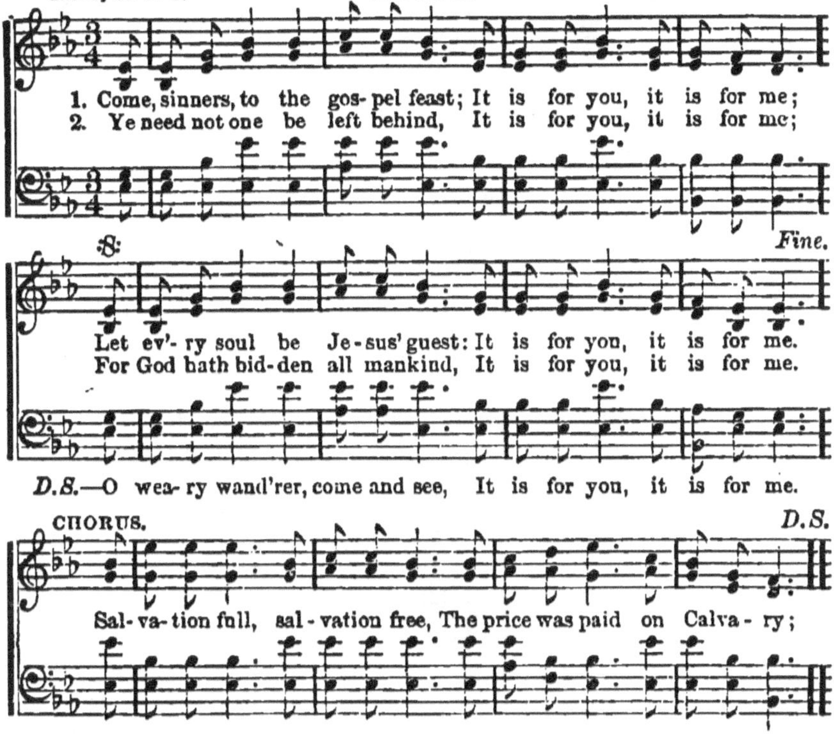

3 Sent by my Lord, on you I call;
  The invitation is to all:
4 Come, all the world! come, sinner, thou!
  All things in Christ are ready now.
5 Come, all ye souls by sin oppressed,
  Ye restless wanderers after rest;
6 Ye poor, and maimed, and halt, and blind
  In Christ a hearty welcome find.

7 My message as from God receive;
  Ye all may come to Christ and live:
8 O let this love your hearts constrain,
  Nor suffer him to die in vain.
9 See him set forth before your eyes,
  That precious, bleeding sacrifice:
10 His offered benefits embrace,
   And freely now be saved by grace.

Copyright, 1889, by H. L. Gilmour.

186. There is a fountain. Key A.

1 There is a fountain ‖: fill'd with blood,:‖
  Drawn from Immanuel's veins,
  And sinners, plunged ‖: beneath that
  Lose all their guilty stains. [flood,:‖
CHO.—Oh, glorious fountain!
    Here will I stay,
    And in thee ever
      Wash my sins away.

2 The dying thief ‖: rejoiced to see :‖
  That fountain in his day,
  And there may I, ‖: though vile as he,:‖
  Wash all my sins away.
3 Thou dying Lamb, ‖: thy precious
  Shall never lose its power, [blood:‖
  Till all the ransomed ‖: Church of God:‖
  Are saved to sin no more.
4 E'er since by faith ‖: I saw the stream :‖
  Thy flowing wounds supply,
  Redeeming love ‖: has been my theme,:‖
  And shall be till I die.

187. By Grace I Will.

  E. E. Hewitt.  Wm. J. Kirkpatrick.

1. Will you go to Jesus now, dear friend? He is calling you to-day;
   Will you seek the bright and better land, By "the true and living way"?
2. Would you know the Saviour's boundless love, And his mercy rich and free?
   Will you seek the saving, cleansing blood, That was shed for you and me.

REFRAIN.

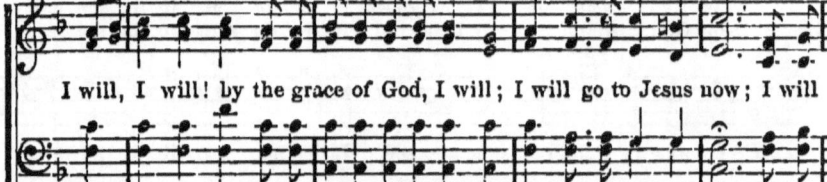

I will, I will! by the grace of God, I will; I will go to Jesus now; I will heed the gospel call, For the promise is for all; I will go to Jesus now.

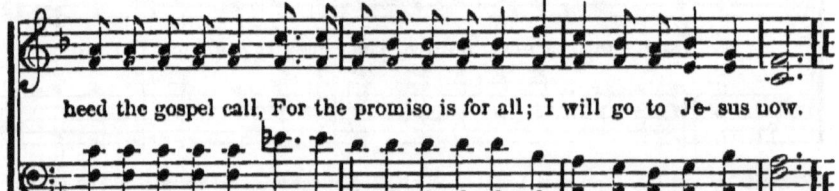

3 Will you consecrate your life to him,
   To be ever his alone?
   And your loving service freely yield,
   To the King upon his throne.

4 Will you follow where the Master leads,
   Choosing only his renown,
   Will you daily bear the cross for him,
   Till he bids you wear the crown?

Copyright, 1883, by Wm. J. Kirkpatrick.

188. Alas! and did.

1 Alas! and did my Saviour bleed?
   And did my Sovereign die?
   Would he devote that sacred head
   For such a worm as I?

2 Was it for crimes that I have done,
   He groaned upon the tree?
   Amazing pity! grace unknown!
   And love beyond degree!

3 Well might the sun in darkness hide,
   And shut his glories in,

When Christ, the mighty Maker, died,
For man, the creature,'s sin.

4 Thus might I hide my blushing face
   While his dear cross appears;
   Dissolve my heart in thankfulness,
   And melt mine eyes to tears.

5 But drops of grief can ne'er repay
   The debt of love I owe:
   Here, Lord, I give myself away,—
   'Tis all that I can do. —I. Watts.

FAMILIAR HYMNS.

189   Just as I am.

1 JUST as I am, without one plea,
But that thy blood was shed for me,
And that thou bidst me come to thee,
O Lamb of God, I come!

Cho.—We're kneeling at the mercy seat;
Where Jesus answers prayer.

2 Just as I am, and waiting not
To rid my soul of one dark blot,
To thee whose blood can cleanse each spot,
O Lamb of God, I come!

3 Just as I am, though tossed about
With many a conflict, many a doubt,
Fightings within, and fears without,
O Lamb of God, I come!

4 Just as I am—poor, wretched, blind;
Sight, riches, healing of the mind,
Yea, all I need, in thee to find,
O Lamb of God, I come!

5 Just as I am—thou wilt receive,
Wilt welcome, pardon, cleanse, relieve;
Because thy promise I believe,
O Lamb of God, I come.

6 Just as I am—thy love unknown
Hath broken every barrier down;
Now, to be thine, yea, thine alone,
O Lamb of God, I come!

190   The Child of a King.

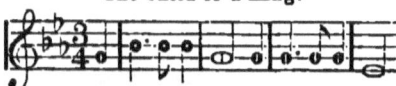

1 MY Father is rich in houses and lands,
He holdeth the wealth of the world in his hands!
Of rubies and diamonds, of silver and gold
His coffers are full,—he has riches untold.

Cho.—I'm the child of a King,
The child of a King;
With Jesus my Saviour
I'm the child of a King.

2 My Father's own Son, the Saviour of men;
Once wandered o'er earth as the poorest of them,
But now he is reigning forever on high,
And will give me a home in heaven by and by.

3 I once was an outcast stranger on earth,
A sinner by choice, an alien by birth! [down,—
But I've been adopted, my name's written
An heir to a mansion, a robe, and a crown.

4 A tent or a cottage, why should I care?
They're building a palace for me over there!
Though exiled from home, yet still I may sing:
All glory to God, I'm the child of a King.

191   The Great Physician.

1 THE great Physician now is here,
The sympathizing Jesus:
He speaks the drooping heart to cheer,
Oh, hear the voice of Jesus.

Cho.—Sweetest note in seraph song,
Sweetest name on mortal tongue,
Sweetest carol ever sung,
Jesus, blessed Jesus.

2 Your many sins are all forgiven,
Oh, hear the voice of Jesus;
Go on your way in peace to heaven,
And wear a crown with Jesus.

3 All glory to the dying Lamb!
I now believe in Jesus;
I love the blessed Saviour's name,
I love the name of Jesus.

4 The children too, both great and small,
Who love the name of Jesus,
May now accept the gracious call
To work and live for Jesus.

5 Come, brethren, help me sing his praise,
Oh, praise the name of Jesus;
Come, sisters, all your voices raise,
Oh, bless the name of Jesus.

6 His name dispels my guilt and fear,
No other name but Jesus;
Oh, how my soul delights to hear
The precious name of Jesus.

7 And when to that bright world above,
We rise to see our Jesus,
We'll sing around the throne of love
His name, the name of Jesus.

192   Blessed Assurance.

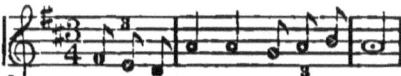

1 BLESSED assurance, Jesus is mine!
Oh, what a foretaste of glory divine!
Heir of salvation, purchased of God,
Born of his Spirit, washed in his blood.

Cho.—This is my story, this is my song,
Praising the Saviour all the day long.

2 Perfect submission, perfect delight,
Visions of rapture burst forth on my sight,
Angels descending, bring from above,
Echoes of mercy, whispers of love.

3 Perfect submission, all is at rest,
I in my Saviour am happy and blest,
Watching and waiting, and looking above,
Filled with his goodness, lost in his love.

193   He Leadeth Me!

1 HE leadeth me! O blessed thought!
O words with heavenly comfort fraught!
Whate'er I do, where'er I be,
Still 'tis God's hand that leadeth me.

Cho.—He leadeth me, he leadeth me,
By his own hand he leadeth me:
His faithful follower I would be,
For by his hand he leadeth me.

2 Sometimes 'mid scenes of deepest gloom,
Sometimes where Eden's bowers bloom,
By waters still, o'er troubled sea,—
Still 'tis his hand that leadeth me!

3 Lord, I would clasp thy hand in mine,
Nor ever murmur nor repine,
Content, whatever lot I see,
Since 'tis my God that leadeth me!

194   Rise, My Soul.

1 RISE, my soul, and stretch thy wings,
Thy better portion trace;
Rise from transitory things
Toward heaven, thy native place:
Sun, and moon, and stars decay;
Time shall soon this earth remove;
Rise, my soul, and haste away
To seats prepared above.

2 Rivers to the ocean run,
Nor stay in all their course;
Fire ascending seeks the sun;
Both speed them to their source:
So a soul that's born of God,
Pants to view his glorious face;
Upward tends to his abode,
To rest in his embrace.

3 Cease, ye pilgrims, cease to mourn,
Press onward to the prize;
Soon our Saviour will return
Triumphant in the skies:
There we'll join the heavenly train,
Welcomed to partake the bliss;
Fly from sorrow, care, and pain,
To realms of endless peace.

195   Blest be the tie.

1 BLEST be the tie that binds
Our hearts in Christian love;
The fellowship of kindred minds
Is like to that above.

2 Before our Father's throne
We pour our ardent prayers;
Our fears, our hopes, our aims are one,
Our comforts and our cares.

3 We share our mutual woes,
Our mutual burdens bear;
And often for each other flows
The sympathising tear.

4 When we asunder part
It gives us inward pain;
But we shall still be joined in heart,
And hope to meet again.

196   Nearer to Thee.

1 NEARER, my God, to thee!
Nearer to thee,
E'en though it be a cross
That raiseth me;
Still all my song shall be,
Nearer, my God, to thee,
Nearer to thee!

2 Though like the wanderer,
The sun gone down,
Darkness be over me,
My rest a stone,
Yet in my dreams I'd be,
Nearer, my God, to thee,
Nearer to thee!

3 There let the way appear
Steps unto heaven;
All that thou sendest me
In mercy given;
Angels to beckon me
Nearer, my God, to thee,
Nearer to thee!

197   Sweet Hour of Prayer.

1 Sweet hour of prayer, sweet hour of prayer,
That calls me from a world of care,
And bids me at my Father's throne
Make all my wants and wishes known!
In seasons of distress and grief
My soul has often found relief,
And oft escaped the tempter's snare
By thy return, sweet hour of prayer.

2 Sweet hour of prayer, sweet hour of prayer,
Thy wings shall my petition bear
To him, whose truth and faithfulness
Engage the waiting soul to bless;
And since he bids me seek his face,
Believe his word, and trust his grace,
I'll cast on him my every care,
And wait for thee, sweet hour of prayer.

Willoughby. C. P. M.

198
But can it be.

1 But can it be that I should prove
Forever faithful to thy love,
From sin forever cease?
I thank thee for the blessed hope;
It lifts my drooping spirits up;
It gives me back my peace.

2 In thee, O Lord, I put my trust,
Mighty, and merciful, and just;
Thy sacred word is passed;
And I, who dare thy word believe,
Without committing sin shall live,
Shall live to God at last.

3 I rest in thy almighty power.
The name of Jesus is my tower
That hides my life above:
Thou canst, thou wilt, my helper be;
My confidence is all in thee,
The faithful God of love.

4 Wherefore, in never-ceasing prayer,
My soul to thy continual care
I faithfully commend;   [save,
Assured that thou through life wilt
And show thyself beyond the grave
My everlasting Friend.

199
O could I speak.

1 O could I speak the matchless worth,
O could I sound the glories forth,
Which in my Saviour shine,
I'd soar and touch the heavenly strings,
And vie with Gabriel while he sings
In notes almost divine.

2 I'd sing the precious blood he spilt,
My ransom from the dreadful guilt
Of sin, and wrath divine;
I'd sing his glorious righteousness,
In which all-perfect, heavenly dress
My soul shall ever shine.

3 I'd sing the characters he bears,
And all the forms of love he wears,
Exalted on his throne;
In loftiest songs of sweetest praise,
I would to everlasting days
Make all his glories known.

4 Well, the delightful day will come
When my dear Lord will bring me
And I shall see his face;   [home,
Then with my Saviour, Brother, Friend,
A blest eternity I'll spend,
Triumphant in his grace.

200
O glorious hope.

1 O glorious hope of perfect love!
It lifts me up to things above;
It bears on eagle's wings.
It gives my ravished soul a taste,
And makes me for some moments feast
With Jesus' priests and kings.

2 Rejoicing now in earnest hope,
I stand and from the mountain top
See all the land below.
Rivers of milk and honey rise,
And all the fruits of Paradise
In endless plenty grow.

3 A land of corn, and wine, and oil,
Favored with God's peculiar smile,
With every blessing blest.   [ness,
There dwells the Lord our Righteous-
And keeps his own in perfect peace,
And everlasting rest.

4 O that I might at once go up;
No more on this side Jordan stop,
But now the land possess;
This moment end my legal years,
Sorrows and sins, and doubts and fears,
A howling wilderness!

201. When I can Read.
Tune, PISGAH. C. M.

1. When I can read my ti-tle clear To mansions in the skies,
CHO.—Then you'll sing halle - lu - jah, And I'll sing hal-le - lu - jah,

I'll bid fare-well to ev'-ry fear, And wipe my weep-ing eyes.
And-we'll all sing hal-le-lu - jah, In that bright world a-bove.

2 Should earth against my soul engage,
And fiery darts be hurled,
Then I can smile at Satan's rage,
And face a frowning world.

3 Let cares like a wild deluge come,
Let storms of sorrow fall,
So I but safely reach my home,
My God, my heaven, my all.

4 There I shall bathe my weary soul
In seas of heavenly rest,
And not a wave of trouble roll
Across my peaceful breast.

202. Jesus, Lover of my soul.

1 JESUS, Lover of my soul,
Let me to thy bosom fly,
While the nearer waters roll,
While the tempest still is high!
Hide me, O my Saviour, hide,
Till the storm of life is past;
Safe into the haven guide,
Oh, receive my soul at last!

2 Other refuge have I none;
Hangs my helpless soul on thee:
Leave, oh, leave me not alone,
Still support and comfort me:
All my trust on thee is stayed,
All my help from thee I bring;
Cover my defenseless head
With the shadow of thy wing!

3 Thou, O Christ, art all I want;
More than all in thee I find;
Raise the fallen, cheer the faint,
Heal the sick, and lead the blind.
Just and holy is thy name,
I am all unrighteousness:
False and full of sin I am,
Thou art full of truth and grace.

4 Plenteous grace with thee is found,
Grace to cover all my sin:
Let the healing streams abound;
Make and keep me pure within.
Thou of life the fountain art,
Freely let me take of thee:
Spring thou up within my heart,
Rise to all eternity. —C. WESLEY

203. All hail the power of Jesus' name!

1 ALL hail the power of Jesus' name!
Let angels prostrate fall;
Bring forth the royal diadem,
And crown him Lord of all.

2 Crown him, ye morning stars of light,
Who fixed this earthly ball;
Now hail the strength of Israel's might,
And crown him Lord of all.

3 Ye chosen seed of Israel's race,
Ye ransomed from the fall,
Hail him who saves you by his grace,
And crown him Lord of all.

4 Sinners, whose love can ne'er forget
The wormwood and the gall,
Go, spread your trophies at his feet,
And crown him Lord of all.

5 Let every kindred, every tribe,
On this terrestrial ball,
To him all majesty ascribe,
And crown him Lord of all.

6 O that with yonder sacred throng
We at his feet may fall!
We'll join the everlasting song,
And crown him Lord of all.

FAMILIAR HYMNS.

204 I hear the Saviour say.

1 I HEAR the Saviour say,
  Thy strength indeed is small,
  Child of weakness, watch and pray,
  Find in me thine all in all.

Cho.—Jesus paid it all,
  All to him I owe,
  Sin had left a crimson stain;
  He washed it white as snow.

2 Lord, now indeed I find
  Thy power, and thine alone,
  Can change this heart of mine,
  And make it all thine own.

3 For nothing good have I
  Whereby thy grace to claim,—
  I'll wash my garment white
  In the blood of Calv'ry's Lamb.

4 Then down beneath the cross
  I lay my sin sick soul,
  I'm counting all but dross
  Thy blood now makes me whole.

205 Are you washed?

1 HAVE you been to Jesus for the cleansing power?
  Are you washed in the blood of the Lamb?
  Are you fully trusting in his grace this hour?
  Are you washed in the blood of the Lamb?

Cho.—Are you washed in the blood,
  In the soul-cleansing blood of the Lamb?
  Are your garments spotless? are they white as snow?
  Are you washed in the blood of the Lamb?

2 Are you walking daily by the Saviour's side?
  Are you washed in the blood of the Lamb?
  Do you rest each moment in the Crucified?
  Are you washed in the blood of the Lamb?

3 When the Bridegroom cometh will your robes be white,
  Pure and white in the blood of the Lamb?
  Will your soul be ready for the mansions bright,
  Are you washed in the blood of the Lamb?

4 Lay aside the garments that are stained with sin,
  And be washed in the blood of the Lamb!
  There's a fountain flowing for the soul unclean,
  O be washed in the blood of the Lamb!

206 I will sprinkle.

1 YE who know your sins forgiven,
  And are happy in the Lord,
  Have you read that gracious promise,
  Which is left upon record!

Cho.—I will sprinkle you with water,
  I will cleanse you from all sin,
  Sanctify and make you holy,
  I will dwell and reign within.

2 Though you have much peace and comfort,
  Greater things you yet may find,
  Freedom from unholy tempers,
  Freedom from the carnal mind.

3 Be as holy, and as happy,
  And as useful here below,
  As it is your Father's pleasure;
  Jesus, only Jesus know.

4 Spread, oh, spread the joyful tidings,
  Tell, oh, tell what God has done,
  Till the nations are conformed
  To the image of his Son.

5 O, may every soul be filled
  With the Holy Ghost to-day;
  He is coming, he is coming;
  O, prepare, prepare the way.

207 I am coming to the cross.

1 I AM coming to the cross,
  I am poor and weak and blind;
  I am counting all but dross,
  I shall full salvation find.

Cho.—I am trusting, Lord, in thee;
  Bless'd Lamb of Calvary;
  Humbly at the cross I bow;
  Jesus saves me—saves me now.

2 Long my heart has sighed for thee,
  Long has evil dwelt within;
  Jesus sweetly speaks to me;
  "I will cleanse you from all sin."

3 Here I give my all to thee,
  Friends, and time, and earthly store,
  Soul and body, thine to be—
  Wholly thine for evermore.

4 In the promises I trust,
  In the cleansing blood confide;
  I am prostrate in the dust,
  I with Christ am crucified.

5 Jesus comes, he fills my soul,
  Perfected in him I am,
  I am every whit made whole,
  Glory, glory to the Lamb!—

208 O tell me no more.

I'll drink when I'm dry, I'll drink a supply, I'll drink from the fountain That never runs dry.

1 O TELL me no more
  Of this world's vain store,
The time for such trifles
  With me now is o'er;
A country I've found
  Where true joys abound,
To dwell I'm determined
  On that happy ground.

2 The souls that believe
  In paradise live,
And me in that number
  Will Jesus receive;
My soul, don't delay;
He calls thee away;
Rise, follow thy Saviour,
  And bless the glad day.

3 No mortal doth know
  What he can bestow,—
What light, strength, and com-
  Go after him, go;   [fort,—
Lo, onward I move
  To a city above,
None guesses how wondrous
  My journey will prove.

4 Great spoils I shall win
  From death, hell, and sin,
'Midst outward afflictions
  Shall feel Christ within:
And when I'm to die,
  "Receive me," I'll cry,
For Jesus hath loved me,
  I cannot tell why:

5 But this I do find,
  We two are so joined,
He'll not live in glory
  And leave me behind:
So this is the race
  I'm running through grace,
Henceforth, till admitted
  To see my Lord's face.

6 And now I'm in care
  My neighbors may share
These blessings: to seek them
  Will none of you dare?
In bondage, O why,
  And death will you lie,
When one here assures you
  Free grace is so nigh?

209 Oh, how happy are they.

Oh, how happy, how happy are they, Oh, how happy, how happy are they, Oh, how

happy are they Who the Saviour obey, And have laid up their treasures above.

OH, how happy are they
  Who the Saviour obey,
And have laid up their treasures above;
  Tongue can never express
  The sweet comfort and peace
Of a soul in its earliest love.

2 That sweet comfort was mine,
  When the favor divine
I received thro' the blood of the Lamb;
  When my heart first believed,
  What a joy I received—
What a heaven in Jesus' name!

3 'Twas a heaven below
  My Redeemer to know,
And the angels could do nothing more
  Than to fall at his feet,
  And the story repeat,
And the Lover of sinners adore.

4 Jesus, all the day long,
  Was my joy and my song;
Oh, that all his salvation might see:
  He hath loved me, I cried,
  He hath suffered and died,
To redeem even rebels like me.

Blessing Invoked.   L. M.   Thanks Returned.

Be present at our table, Lord,
Be here as everywhere adored,
Thy creatures bless, and grant that we
May feast in Paradise with thee.

We thank thee, Lord, for this our food,
But more because of Jesus' blood;
Let manna to our souls be given,—
The Bread of Life sent down from heaven.

The above was used by John Wesley at the table.

INDEX.

	HYMN.		HYMN.		HYMN.
A charge to keep I have	20	COMPANIONSHIP WITH.	79	I have surrendered to	144
A glad new song of peace	61	Consecrate me now, Je-	49	I heard a voice in tones	174
Alas! and did my Sav-.	188	CROWNING JESUS,	58	I hear the Saviour say	204
All glory to Jesus, I'll	106			I know a fountain deep	91
All hail the power of Je-	203	Day is done, night has	158	I'LL BE THERE,	148
All praise to him who	92	Dear Jesus, I long to be	145		
ALWAY,	153	Down at the cross, on	101	I love my Saviour, his	87
Am I a soldier of the	155	Down at the cross, where	149	I love thee, my Saviour,	93
Amid a world of sin,	110	Draw me close to thy	80	"I'M A LOST MAN,"	176
A mother's voice is call-	165			I'm lost! I'm lost! the	176
An army is coming, their	19	Enthroned on high, al-.	39	I'm more than con-	107
And can it be that I	73	Equip me for the war,	22	I'm on my way to glory	104
And can I yet delay?	182			I'm walking now in	153
Are you ready for the	112	FILL ME NOW,	31	I'm weary of this load	51
Arise, my soul, arise,	94	Fly to the rescue, dan-.	18	In ev'ry tribe and ev'ry.	164
ARISE, SHINE,	85	Forest, L. M.,	55	IN HIS KINGDOM,.	95
Arm for he battle of glo-	3	For Jesus' sake I sold	113	IN HIS NAME,	7
A ship in wind and storm	130	FOR YOU AND ME,	166	In the morning when the	86
A stream from Calv'ry's.	128	FRIENDS, NOT SERVANT	78	In thy cleft, O Rock of.	131
AT THE CROSS.	53	From ev'ry stormy wind	142	INVOCATION,	26
At the fount I stand,	77	FULL OF GLORY, .	115	I praise the Lord when.	116
Away from my Father, .	170	FULL SALVATION,	139	I saw a blood-washed	81
Away, my unbelieving	74			I thirst, thou wounded .	57
Azmon, C. M.,	39	Gather them in at the	8	IT IS WELL WITH MY	122
		GIVE ME THY PERFECT	48		
Bartimeus, 8, 7.,	181	GLORIOUS VICTORY,	12	I've reached the land of	125
Behold a stranger in the	156	GLORY TO GOD, HALLE-	83	I will sing of a time,	95
BEHOLD THE BRIDE-	112	Glory to God I redeemed	5	I WILL SPRINKLE,	206
Behold! the Lamb of	151	God calling yet I shall I.	179	I worship thee, O Holy.	42
Be present at our table, .	210	GRACE IS FREE,	175		
BEULAH LAND,	125	Gracious Spirit, love di-	33	JESUS COMES,	117
Blessed assurance, Jesus	192			Jesus is good to me,	87
BLESSED BE THE NAME	92	HALLELUJAH! AMEN, .	63	JESUS IS STRONG TO DE-	67
		HAPPY DAY,	99	Jesus is the light, the	121
		Hark! hark! loud, long	1	Jesus, lover of my 202,	102
BLESSED REDEEMER, .	97	Have you been to Jesus	205	Jesus my all to heaven,	90
Blest be the tie that binds	195	HEALING FOR THEE, .	157	Jesus my life, thyself	31
BLOW THE TRUMPET, .	4	HE CAME TO SAVE ME,	100	JESUS SAVES,	86
Boyleston, S. M.,	35	He leadeth me! O bless-	193	Jesus shall reign where-	132
Bravely launch the temp-	6	HELP DRAWETH NEAR,	19	Jesus the Saviour is pass-	157
Breathe thou upon us, .	26	Here in thy name we are	143	Jesus! the very thought	72
Buried with Christ and .	47	HE SPEAKETH, " PEACE	158	Jesus, thine all victori-	40
But can it be that I	198	HE THAT OVERCOMETH	84	JUST AHEAD,	150
By faith I view my Sav-	152	HIDE THOU ME, .	131	Just as I am, without	189
BY GRACE I WILL,	187	HIS YOKE IS EASY,	135		
		Ho! every one that is	172	Laban, S. M.,	20
Can a mother forget the	71	HOLINESS,	138	Late at night I saw the.	111
CLEANSE AND FILL ME,	46	Holy Ghost, with light	34	LET THE KING COME	72
Come, all who are thirsty	169	HOLY SPIRIT, COME, .	28	Let us give the cup of	7
Come, all ye saints, sa-.	58	HOSANNA TO OUR KING	120	Lift your heads! lift	98
Come, believer, hung'ring	159	Hover o'er me, Holy	31	LIGHT OF MY LIFE,	80
Come, every soul by sin	162	How firm a foundation,	70	Lord God, the Holy	35
Come, Holy Ghost! to .	25	How oft in holy con-	63	Lord, I am thine, entire-	56
Come, Holy Spirit, come	36			Lord, I care not for rich-	183
Come, Holy Spirit, raise	37	I am coming, Jesus,	46	Lord, I hear of showers	140
Come, sinners, to the	185	I am coming to the cross	207	Lord, we come before	52
Come, thou fount of every	160	I am walking in the light	138		
Come thou into the ark of	178	If you want pardon,	139	MEET ME THERE,	173
Come, ye sinners, poor .	181	I have a blessed hope to-	69	'Mid the toil and the	150
COMFORTER,	29	I have heard of a land,	89	MIGHTY ROCK, .	44

THE SILVER TRUMPET.

MISSING, . . . 111	REDEEMED, . . . 141	There's a city that looks 66
MORE FAITH IN JESUS, 62	REDEEMED, PRAISE . 119	There's a great day . 168
Mortal tongue cannot, . 45	Redeeming love! how . 171	There's a message from. 167
MY BELOVED, . . 102	Rise, my soul, and . 194	There's nothing like the. 175
My body, soul and spirit, 60	*Rockingham*, L. M., . 37	There's sunshine in my. 103
My Father is rich in . 190	Rock of Ages! cleft for. 44	The Saviour died for me 166
MY FATHER'S AT THE. 130	Round Christ the great 126	THE SILVER TRUMPET, 1
My soul, be on thy . 21		THE SPIRIT AND THE . 163
My soul's full of glory,. 137	SALVATION FULL AND. 164	THE STRANGER AT THE 156
	SALVATION'S RIVER, . 101	THE TEMP. LIFE-BOAT, 6
Nearer, my God, to thee 196	Saviour, breathe thy ho-. 29	THE WATER OF LIFE, . 118
NOTHING BUT THE LIV- 184	*Sessions*, L. M., . . 32	Though my sins were . 118
Now I feel the sacred . 30	SETTING ME FREE, . 106	THOU WAST SMITTEN, . 146
	SHOWERS OF BLESSING, 143	'Tis long since Jesus . 48
O could I speak the . 199	Sing all the way to Zion 96	To him that overcometh, 84
O for a heart to praise . 127	Sing on, ye joyful pil- . 76	TO THEE, O LORD, I . 50
O for that flame of liv- 32	SINGING, GLORY, . . 104	TO THE WORLD I'M . 45
O glorious hope of per- 200	Soldiers of the cross, a-. 17	To thy cross, dear Christ 129
O happy day, that fixed 99	SONS OF GOD, MARCH . 2	
O happy day! what a . 119	Sowing in the morning, . 13	UNDER HIS WINGS, . 65
Oh, blessed fellowship . 79	Speak to me, Jesus, I'm 123	UNSEARCHABLE RICH-. 124
Oh, come to the merci-. 163	SPEED ON! . . . 11	
Oh, glad "whosoever," . 141	Spirit of burning! quick 24	Vain, delusive world, a-. 54
Oh, how blessed is the . 78	Stand up, stand up for . 15	VICTORY! . . . 52
Oh, how happy are they 209	STANDING ON THE PR 82	
Oh, I have found him . 97	SUNSHINE IN THE SOUL, 103	WASHED IN THE . . 105
Oh, lift your heads ye . 120	SURRENDERED, . . 144	WASHED WHITE AS . 118
Oh, now I see the cleans- 136	Sweet hour of prayer, . 197	Wast thou smitten, wast 146
Oh, rally round the stan- 9	Sweet is my hiding place 65	Watchman, blow the . 4
Oh, the joy of the Lord 64		Watch, ye saints, with . 117
Oh, turn ye, oh, turn ye, 161	Take courage, temp- . 11	WE ARE GOING HOME, . 90
Oh, what joy and peace 105	Take my life, and let it. 43	We are never, never . 83
O Jesus, Lord, thy dy-. 53	Thank God for a perfect 133	We'll never lay down . 12
O Lamb of God! to . 50	THE BEAUTIFUL LIGHT 121	We'll sound the loud . 137
O, my soul is full of glo- 115	The blood's applied! my 154	We thank thee, Lord, . 210
ONLY TRUST HIM, . 162	THE BLOOD-WASHED . 81	What a Friend we have . 94
ON THE CROSS, . . 151	The Bridegroom cometh 98	What can sweetly fill my 184
On the happy, golden . 173	THE CITY OF GOLD, . 66	What poor despised . 147
Onward, Christain sol- . 10	THE CLEANSING BLOOD 126	WHAT WILL THE FIRST 89
Onward marching, who, 23	The cross! the cross! . 134	What wondrous love is . 108
O REST, SWEET REST, . 133	THE FIRM FOUNDA- . 70	When I can read my ti- 201
O sinner, come, there's . 177	THE GOSPEL FEAST, . 185	When in the tempest . 67
O Spirit of the living . 38	The great physician now 191	When I survey the won- 59
O tell me no more, . 208	THE HAVEN OF REST, 75	When Jesus laid his . 100
O that my load of sin . 55	Thy Holy Spirit, Lord, . 27	When peace, like a riv-. 122
O the unsearchable rich- 124	THE JOY OF THE LORD, 64	WHERE IS MY CHILD?. 165
O thou in whose pres- . 114	THY KING COMETH, . 68	While struggling thro' . 62
O ye wand'rers, come to 180	THE KING OF GLORY, . 23	WHY DON'T YOU COME 180
	The Lord is my Shep- . 135	WHY WILT THOU DIE? 174
Penitence, . . . 54	The Lord shall arise, . 85	*Willoughby*, C. P. M., . 198
PENTECOST, . . . 24	THE MERCY-SEAT, . 142	WILL YOU COME? . 167
Pisgah, C. M., . . 201	THE MORNING DRAW-. 9	Will you go to Jesus, . 187
Pleyel's Hymn, 7s., . 33	The morning light is . 14	With hosannas loud . 68
Portuguese Hymn, . 70	THE PRODIGAL'S RE- . 170	Work, for the night is . 16
Praise the Lord, praise . 88	There is a fountain filled 186	
Precious Jesus, Saviour. 28	There is a land of pure. 148	Ye sons of God, awake,. 2
PRECIOUS STREAM, . 128	There is a spot to me . 109	Ye who know your sins . 206

www.ingramcontent.com/pod-product-compliance
Lightning Source LLC
Chambersburg PA
CBHW030304170426
43202CB00009B/864